THE PO
POSITIVE
FOR YOUNG PEOPLE

By

Norman Vincent Peale

A Cedar Book
No. 110

WORLD'S WORK LTD
KINGSWOOD TADWORTH SURREY

Also by Norman Vincent Peale

A GUIDE TO CONFIDENT LIVING
THE POWER OF POSITIVE THINKING
THE AMAZING RESULTS OF POSITIVE THINKING
STAY ALIVE ALL YOUR LIFE
THE TOUGH-MINDED OPTIMIST
INSPIRING MESSAGES FOR DAILY LIVING
THE COMING OF THE KING (for children)
ADVENTURES IN THE HOLY LAND
JESUS OF NAZARETH
SIN, SEX AND SELF-CONTROL
ENTHUSIASM MAKES THE DIFFERENCE
THE NEW ART OF LIVING
YOU CAN IF YOU THINK YOU CAN

In collaboration with Dr. Smiley Blanton

THE ART OF HAPPINESS
FAITH IS THE ANSWER

Edited by Norman Vincent Peale

FAITH MADE THEM CHAMPIONS
UNLOCK YOUR FAITH POWER

Original American edition published by
Prentice-Hall, Inc., New York,

First published 1955
First published as a Cedar Book 1964
Seventh impression 1977

SBN 437 95110 3

Made and printed in Great Britain by
Richard Clay (The Chaucer Press) Ltd, Bungay, Suffolk

Introduction

THE purpose of this book is a very direct and simple one: to help young people find themselves and live happy and effective lives. It is to describe and demonstrate one of the most important and valuable laws of successful living, "the power of positive thinking."

This volume is a revised and shortened form of my book bearing the same title. It is published in response to the suggestion often made that nothing could happen to a person of greater good fortune than to master the positive thinking technique early in life. Why learn it the hard way after years of failure and unhappiness? How I wish I had learned the creative and dynamic law of positive thinking in my teens! It would have saved me heartaches and prevented failures.

I have selected from many incidents in the lives of people whom I have known, anecdotes and experiences particularly applicable to youthful readers, that they may realise that the same disturbing dilemmas that they face also occur in the lives of others. Also, that even as others have solved their problems, so can they overcome their own difficulties.

This book is a practical, direct-action, personal-improvement manual. It is written with the sole purpose of helping the reader achieve a happy, satisfying, worthwhile life. It tells how to be rid of the inferiority complex, how to get along with people, how to overcome fear, how to get along well in studies or one's job and how to deal successfully with life's problems generally.

I thoroughly and enthusiastically believe in certain demonstrated and effective principles which, when practised, result in a victorious life. My aim is to set them forth in this volume in a logical, simple and understanding manner so that the reader feeling a sense of need may learn a practical method by which he can build for himself, with God's help, the kind of life he desires.

If you read this book thoughtfully, carefully absorbing its teachings, and if you will sincerely and persistently practise the principles and formulas set forth herein, you can experience an amazing improvement within yourself. By using the techniques outlined here you can modify or change the circumstances in which you now live, assuming control over them rather than continuing to be directed by them. Your relations with other people will improve. You will become a more popular, esteemed and well-liked person. By mastering these principles you will enjoy a delightful sense of achievement. You will become more useful and will wield an expanded influence. You may experience a new and keen pleasure in living.

I need not point out that the powerful principles outlined in this book are not my invention, but are given to us by the greatest Teacher who ever lived and Who lives still. This book teaches applied Christianity; a simple yet scientific system of practical techniques of successful living that works.

NORMAN VINCENT PEALE

Contents

CHAPTER 1

Trust Yourself

TRUST yourself. You cannot be successful or happy without confidence in your own powers and abilities. To succeed you need self-confidence. The inferiority complex prevents the attainment of your hopes, but self-confidence leads to successful achievement. Such a mental attitude is extremely important and this book will help you believe in yourself and release your inner powers. You need no longer suffer from that painful sickness experienced by so many and which is popularly called the inferiority complex. When proper steps are taken—and we shall outline these steps—it can be overcome. You can develop creative faith in yourself, faith that is justified. Believe that, practise these principles and you will feel like a new person, for in fact you will be a new person.

I had spoken at a school commencement and afterward the president of the class came to me and asked, "May I talk with you about a matter of desperate importance to me?"

"Where can we talk?" I asked him. After all the others had gone we settled for the stairs leading down from the stage to the empty auditorium.

"I'm seeing a man tomorrow about a job," the boy told me in an anxious tone. "It's something I want, and if he doesn't like me or think I'm good enough for it, my whole life will be ruined."

I suggested that he relax a little, that nothing was quite that final. But he didn't go along with that.

"I have a terrible disbelief in myself," he said dejectedly. "I just know I can't put it over: I'm absolutely sunk." Even though he was so well liked and capable that he had been elected class president, still he had no faith in himself.

"It's important to discover why you have this feeling of self-distrust," I said, "but that will take time. To pull you through this immediate problem I am going to give you a formula which will work if you use it."

"I'll do anything," the boy promised.

"Very well," I said. "As you walk home tonight repeat the words I am going to give you over and over. Repeat them after you have gone to bed. When you awaken tomorrow morning, repeat them before you get up. Say them on the way to your appointment about the job.

"Do this with an attitude of faith. And if you practise believing, you will receive sufficient strength to deal with this interview. You will conduct yourself effectively and your best qualities will show up well. Later if you wish we can go into the basic problem of your lack of self-confidence to solve that problem permanently.

"The words you are to repeat are these: 'I can do all things through Christ which strengtheneth me.' " (Philippians 4:13) He was unfamiliar with the passage so I wrote it out for him on a card and had him read it over to me several times.

He pulled himself up; stood quietly for a moment; then said with considerable feeling. "O.K., Doctor, O.K. I get the idea."

The next afternoon he telephoned me and announced jubilantly that he had the job, adding, "Isn't it fantastic that a few words from the Bible could do so much for me?"

I replied, "The practice of positive thinking is one of the greatest laws of successful living. You are indeed fortunate to learn it early in life."

This boy came to me later and we went into the reasons for his inferiority attitudes. They were cleared away by the application of scientific personal counselling and religious faith. Gradually he attained a strong, steady, reasonable confidence. His personality has taken on a positive, not a negative, character, so that he no longer repels success but, on the contrary, draws it to him. He now has authentic confidence in his own powers.

There are various causes of inferiority feelings, and not a few stem from childhood.

An executive consulted me about a young man whom he wished to advance in his company. "But," he explained, "he cannot be trusted with important confidential information and I'm sorry, for otherwise I would make him my administrative assistant. He has all the other necessary qualifications, but he talks too much, and without meaning to do so, tells matters of a private and important nature."

Upon analysis I found that he "talked too much" simply because of an inferiority feeling. To compensate for this, he gave into the temptation of parading his knowledge.

In his job, he associated with young men who were rather well-to-do, all of whom had attended college and belonged to fraternities. But this boy was reared in poverty, had not been a college man or a fraternity member. Thus he felt himself inferior to his associates in education and social background. To build himself up with his associates and to enhance his self-esteem, his subconscious mind (as is customary) sought to provide a compensatory mechanism and supplied him with a means of raising his ego.

He was on "the inside" in the industry, and accompanied his superior to conferences where he met outstanding men and listened to important private conversations. He reported just enough of his "inside information" to cause his associates to regard him with admiration and envy. This served to elevate his self-esteem and satisfy his desire for recognition.

When the employer became aware of the cause of this personality trait, being a kindly and understanding man, he pointed out to his young assistant the opportunities in business to which his abilities could lead him. He also described how his inferiority feelings caused his unreliability in confidential matters. This self-knowledge, together with a sincere practising of the techniques of faith and prayer, helped the young man to became a valuable asset to his company. His real powers were released.

I can perhaps illustrate the manner in which many young people acquire an inferiority complex through the use of a personal reference. As a small boy I was painfully thin. I had lots of energy, was on a track team, was healthy and hard as nails, but thin. And that bothered me because I didn't want to be thin. I wanted to be fat. I was called "skinny," but I didn't want to be called "skinny." I wanted to be called "fat." I longed to be hard-boiled and tough and fat. I did everything to get fat. I drank cod-liver oil, consumed vast numbers of milk shakes, ate thousands of chocolate sundaes with whipped cream and nuts, cakes and pies innumerable, but they did not affect me in the slightest. I stayed thin and lay awake at night thinking and agonising about it. I kept on trying to get heavy until I was about thirty, when all of a sudden did I get heavy? I bulged at the seams. Then I became self-conscious because I was so fat, and finally had to take off forty pounds with equal agony to get myself down to respectable size.

In the second place (to conclude this personal analysis which I give only because it may help others by showing how this malady works), I was a minister's son and was constantly reminded of that fact. Everybody else could do everything, but if I did even the slightest little thing—"Ah, you are a preacher's son." So I didn't want to be a preacher's son, for preachers' sons are supposed to be super nice and namby-pamby. I wanted to be known as a hard-boiled guy. Perhaps that is why preachers' sons get their reputation for being a little difficult, because they rebel against having to carry the banner of the church all the time. I vowed there was one thing I would never do, and that was to become a preacher.

Also, I came of a family practically every member of which was a performer in public, a platform speaker, and that was the last thing I wanted to be. They used to make me get up in public to make speeches when it scared me to death, even filled me with terror. That was years ago, but the twinge of it comes to me every now and then when I walk on to a platform. I had to use every known device to develop confidence in what powers the good Lord gave me.

I found the solution of this problem in the simple techniques of faith taught in the Bible. These principles can release the powers which have been stifled by a feeling of inadequacy, a malady which may arise from some emotional violence done to us in childhood, or be the consequence of something we did to ourselves.

Perhaps you have an older brother who is a brilliant student. Gets As in school: you make only Cs, and you never hear the last of it. So you believe that you can never succeed in life as he can. He gets As and you get Cs; so you reason that you are consigned to getting Cs all your life. Apparently you do not realise that some of those failing to get high grades in school have been the greatest successes outside of school. Just because somebody gets an A in college doesn't make him the greatest man in the country, because maybe his As will stop when he gets his diploma, and the fellow who gets Cs in school will go on later to get the real As in life.

The greatest secret for eliminating the inferiority complex, which is another term for deep and profound self-doubt, is to fill your mind to overflowing with faith. Develop a tremendous faith in God and that will give you a humble yet soundly realistic faith in yourself.

The acquiring of dynamic faith is accomplished by prayer, lots of prayer, by reading and mentally absorbing the Bible and by practising its faith techniques. In another chapter I deal with specific formulas or methods of prayer, but I want to point out here that the type of prayer that produces the quality of faith required to eliminate inferiority is of a particular nature. Surface skimming, formalistic and perfunctory prayer are not sufficiently powerful.

A cook in the home of friends of mine in Texas was asked how she so completely mastered her troubles. She answered that ordinary problems could be met by ordinary prayers, but that "when a big trouble comes along, you have to pray deep prayers."

A friend of mine, the late Harlowe B. Andrews of Syracuse, New York, said, "God will rate you according to the size of your prayers." Doubtless he was right, for the Scriptures say, "According to your faith be it unto you." (Matthew 9:29) So the bigger your problem, the bigger your prayers should be.

Roland Hayes, the Negro tenor, quoted to me his grandfather, a man whose education was not equal to that of his grandson, but whose native wisdom was obviously sound. He said, "The trouble with lots of prayers is they ain't got no suction." Drive your prayers deep into your doubts, fears, inferiorities. Pray deep, big prayers that have plenty of suction and you will come up with powerful and vital faith.

Go to a competent spiritual adviser, such as your minister or a teacher who is a genuinely religious person, and let him teach you how to have faith. The ability to possess and utilise faith and gain the release of the powers it provides are skills and, like any skills, must be studied and practised to gain perfection.

One way to learn how to have faith and thereby to build up feelings of self-confidence is the practice of suggesting confidence to your mind. Thought disciplining is important in re-educating your mind and in making a power-producing plant. It is possible to drive confident thoughts into your consciousness until such faith attitudes take over control. Let me tell you about one man who did so by the use of a unique method.

"I'm a travelling salesman," he told me, "and I drive around all day calling on my customers. I used to think thoughts of fear and defeat between calls, and let me tell you, my sales were down. Now I tuck one of these cards into my windshield."

He handed me some cards. One read: "If ye have faith . . . nothing shall be impossible unto you." (Matthew 17:20) And another: "If God be for us, who can be against us?" (Romans 8:31)

He went on. "Since I've been using these cards as I drive and committing the words to memory, the old inferiority and disbelief have gone. It's really wonderful the way this method has changed me. It has helped in my business, too. How did I expect to make a sale when I went into a man's office thinking I was going to fail?"

This man learned a wonderful method for getting rid of inferiority. He was filling his mind with affirmations of the presence and help of God. He actually changed his thought processes by soaking his mind with the most powerful thoughts in this world. His potential powers were set free. Go through the Bible and copy sentences similar to those used by this salesman. Commit them to memory and "drop" them into your conscious mind every day by saying them over many times. They will gradually seep into your subconscious and before you know it will change you.

We build up a feeling of insecurity or security by how we think. If in our thoughts we constantly fix attention upon sinister expectations of dire events that might happen, the result will be a constant feeling of insecurity. And what is even more serious is the tendency to create, by the power of thought, the very condition we fear. This salesman actually created positive results by vital thoughts of courage and confidence through the process of feeding to his mind strong ideas. His powers, curiously inhibited by a defeat psychology, now flower out of a personality in which creative attitudes had been stimulated.

Lack of self-confidence apparently is one of the great problems besetting people today. In a university a survey was made of six hundred students studying psychology courses. The students were asked to state their most difficult personal problem. Seventy-five per cent listed lack of confidence.

The blows of life, the accumulation of difficulties, the multiplication of problems tend to sap energy and leave you "down" and discouraged. For example: a charming young lady of eighteen came into my office one day. She had lost everything, she told me; she had nothing left. "Besides, I have lost all faith," were her words.

I knew her and something of her circumstances. Her father's financial condition was such that he was unable to send his daughter to college as he had promised.

"Suppose you take a piece of paper," I suggested, "and write down some of the values you have left. What about your health?"

"Oh, I'm never sick," she said.

So I wrote down, "Unusually good health."

"Of course there isn't enough food in the house? You often go hungry?" I asked.

She almost giggled. "Nothing like that. A bit of dieting wouldn't hurt me any."

"Comfortably fed and housed," I wrote.

"Your mother and father dislike you and are unkind to you?" was my next suggestion.

"Mother's sweet; and father—he feels dreadfully about disappointing me." She looked at me and flushed. "I guess I've been pretty silly, haven't I?"

With a change in her viewpoint, her mental attitude changed. She now was aware of her splendid assets and stopped thinking negatively about the difficulties. Faith swept away doubts; she had more than enough power to meet the changed conditions of her life.

This incident illustrates a profound truth which is expressed in a very important statement made by the famous psychiatrist Dr. Karl Menninger. He said: "Attitudes are more important than facts." That is worth repeating until its truth grips you. Any fact facing us, however difficult, even seemingly hopeless, is not so important as our attitude towards that fact. How you think about a fact may defeat you before you ever do anything about it. You may permit a fact to overwhelm you mentally before you start to deal with it actually. On the other hand, a confident and optimistic thought pattern can modify or overcome the fact altogether.

I know a baseball coach who, when his team is viewing a coming game pessimistically, employs what he calls "the vacuum-cleaner method" on the boys. By a series of questions he "sucks the dust" out of their minds; draws out their negative attitudes. Then quietly he suggests positive ideas and gives them a new conception of the facts. They all say how differently they feel after this coach has "gone to work" on them. His confident attitude has made the difference. Yet his appraisal of the facts had been objective. His secret is simply to give his team a normal view of the opposition, but slanted to the positive side.

So if you feel that you are defeated and have lost confidence in your ability, sit down, take a piece of paper and make a list, not of the factors that are against you, but of those that are for you. If you or I or anybody thinks constantly of the forces that seem to be against us, we will build them up into a power far beyond that which is justified. They will assume a formidable strength which they do not actually possess. But if, on the contrary, you mentally visualise and affirm and reaffirm your assets and keep your thoughts on them, emphasising them to the fullest extent, you will be able to overcome any difficulty regardless of what it may be. Your inner powers will come to your aid and, with the help of God, lift you from defeat to victory.

One of the most powerful concepts, one which is a sure cure for lack of confidence, is to practise the thought that God is actually with you and helping you. This is one of the simplest teachings in religion, namely, that Almighty God will be your companion, will stand by you, help you, and see you through. No other idea is so powerful in developing self-confidence as this simple belief when practised. To practise it, simply affirm: "God is with me; God is helping me; God is guiding me." Spend several minutes each day visualising His presence. Then practise believing that affirmation. Go about your daily activities on the assumption that what you have affirmed and visualised is true. Affirm it, visualise it, believe it, and it will actualise itself. The release of power which this procedure stimulates will astonish you.

Feelings of confidence depend upon the type of thoughts that habitually occupy your mind. Think defeat and you are bound to feel defeated. But practise thinking confident thoughts, make it a dominating habit, and you will develop such a strong sense of capacity that regardless of what difficulties arise you will be able to overcome them. Feelings of confidence actually induce increased strength. Basil King once said, "Be bold, and mighty forces will come to your aid." Experience proves the truth of this. You will feel these mighty spiritual forces aiding you as your increasing faith reconditions your attitudes from negative to positive.

Emerson declared a tremendous truth, "They conquer who believe they can." And he added, "Do the thing you fear and the death of fear is certain." Practise confidence and faith and your fears and insecurities will soon have no power over you.

Once when the famous Southern General Stonewall Jackson planned a daring attack, one of his generals fearfully objected, saying, "I'm afraid of this" or "I fear that . . ." Putting his hand on his timorous subordinate's shoulder, Jackson said, "General, never take counsel of your fears." How right that is. Never listen to your fears. Listen to your faith.

Fill your mind with thoughts of faith, confidence, and security. This will force out or expel all thoughts of doubt, all lack of confidence. To one man who for a long time had been haunted by insecurities and fears I suggested that he read through the Bible underlining in red pencil every statement it contains relative to courage and confidence. He also committed them to memory, in effect cramming his mind full of the healthiest, happiest, most powerful thoughts in the world. These dynamic thoughts transformed him from a being surrounded by cringing hopelessness to a man of compelling force. The change in just a few weeks was remarkable. From almost complete defeat he emerged a confident and inspiring personality. He now radiates courage and magnetism. He regained confidence in himself and his own powers by a simple process of thought conditioning.

To sum up—what can you do *now* to build up your self-confidence? Following are ten simple, workable rules for overcoming inadequacy attitudes and learning to practise faith. Thousands have used these rules, reporting successful results. Undertake this programme and you, too, will build up confidence in your powers. You, too, will have a new feeling of power. You can be through with your inferiority complex forever.

1. Formulate and stamp indelibly on your mind a mental picture of yourself as succeeding. Hold this picture tenaciously. Never permit it to fade. Your mind will seek to develop this picture. Never think of yourself as failing; never doubt the reality of the mental image of success. The mind always tries to complete what it pictures. So *always* picture "success" no matter how badly things seem to be going at the moment.

2. Whenever a negative thought concerning your personal powers comes to mind, deliberately voice a positive thought to cancel it out.

3. Do not build up obstacles in your imagination. Depreciate every so-called obstacle. Minimise them. Difficulties must be studied and efficiently dealt with

to be eliminated, but they must be seen only for what they are. They must not be inflated by fear thoughts.

4. Do not be awestruck by other people and try to copy them. Nobody can be you as efficiently as YOU can. Remember also that most people, despite their confident appearance and actions, are often as scared as you are and as doubtful of themselves.

5. Ten times a day repeat these dynamic words: "If God be *for* us, who can be against us?" (Stop reading and repeat them NOW slowly and confidently.)

6. Get a competent counsellor to help you understand why you do what you do. Learn the origin of your inferiority and self-doubt feelings which often begin in childhood. Self-knowledge leads to a cure.

7. Ten times each day practise the following affirmation, repeating it out loud if possible. "I can do all things through Christ which strengtheneth me." Repeat those words NOW. That magic statement is the most powerful antidote on earth to inferiority thoughts.

8. Make a true estimate of your own ability, then raise it ten per cent. Do not become egotistical, but develop a wholesome self-respect. Believe in your own God-released powers.

9. Put yourself in God's hands. To do that, simply state, "I am in God's hands." Then believe you are NOW receiving all the power you need. "Feel" it flowing into you. Affirm that "the kingdom of

God is within you" (Luke 17:21) in the form of adequate power to meet life's demands.

10. Remind yourself that God is with you and nothing can defeat you. Believe that you *now* RECEIVE power from Him.

CHAPTER 2

Power Comes from a Quiet Mind

A YOUNG girl, not more than fifteen years old, came to me after church one morning. "Could I ask you something, Dr. Peale?" she said.

I asked her to wait while I shook hands with a long line of people. Then I took her back to my study. "What's the matter?" I asked, expecting to hear about some difficulty at school, either with her friends or with her lessons.

"It's my mother," she said instead. "She can't sleep. I've got to find some way to help her sleep."

I was reminded of an incident that had happened to me, a man who had complained at the breakfast table in a hotel where I was stopping of his inability to sleep. "Maybe the coffee I drank before retiring had something to do with it," he said.

Then another man spoke up. "I had a grand night. Of course," with a twinkle, "I used my go-to-sleep plan, which never fails."

I prodded him for an explanation, as he meant me to do, and he gave me the following as his "never fail go-to-sleep technique."

"When I was a boy, my father, a farmer, had the habit of gathering the family in the parlour at bedtime and he read to us out of the Bible. I can hear him yet. In fact, every time I hear those Bible verses I always seem to hear them in the tone of my father's voice. After prayers I would go up to my room and sleep like a top.

"But when I left home I got away from the Bible reading and prayer habit.

"I must admit that for years practically the only time I ever prayed was when I got into a jam. But some months ago my wife and I, having a number of difficult problems, decided we would try it again. We found it a very helpful practice, so now every night before going to bed she and I together read the Bible and have a little session of prayer. I don't know what there is about it, but I have been sleeping better and things have improved all down the line. In fact, I find it so helpful that even out on the road, as I am now, I still read the Bible and pray. Last night I got into bed and read the 23rd Psalm. I read it out loud and it did me a lot of good."

I told this incident to the girl. She listened carefully.

"I see," she said. "I'll tell mother."

Then she thanked me politely and left. Later she told me that her mother followed this suggestion and "Now she never takes a sleeping pill, and," the girl added, "when I get a bit jittery I try it myself and it's wonderful for quieting the mind."

The essence of the secret of acquiring quietude of mind lies in a change of mental attitude. Probably that mother would have to learn to live on a different thought basis, even though such thought change requires effort. The life of strain is difficult; the life of inner peace is the easiest type of existence for it is harmonious and without tension. The chief factor in gaining mental peace is to revise your thinking and take the relaxed attitude of accepting God's gift of peace.

As an illustration of taking a relaxed attitude and therefore receiving peace of mind, I always think of an experience I had after delivering a lecture one evening. It was late and I was back in my hotel when the telephone rang. Without identifying himself, a young man—I judged him young from his voice—said, "I just wanted you to pray with me. I thought if you would pray with me perhaps I could get some peace."

"Now?" I said, somewhat surprised. "You mean over the telephone?"

"I thought maybe you would," said the boy.

I wanted to ask him what was troubling him, why he needed peace. But it seemed simpler just to do as he asked. When I finished I suggested, "Won't you pray?" There was no response and I thought I heard sobbing. "Go ahead and cry," I said. "And then pray. Simply tell the Lord everything that is bothering you."

Presently he started to pray, hesitantly at first, then he gathered vigour. He poured out a lot of frustration and failure, also many immoral sex practices. Then he added: "Dear God, I have a lot of nerve to ask You to do anything for me, because I never did anything for You. I guess You know what a no-account I am, even though I put on a big front. I am sick of all this, dear God. Please help me."

Then I prayed again. "Lord," I asked, "please help this young man and give him peace." Then I stopped.

There was a long pause. Then I heard him say wonderingly, "Why—why, I feel clean inside and happy and—and—peaceful."

This boy had employed a simple and workable technique for having a peaceful mind. He emptied his mind of all that was disturbing him; and then he received peace as a gift from God.

As a physician said, "Many of my patients have nothing wrong with them except their thoughts. So I have a favourite prescription that I write for some. But it is not a prescription that you can fill in a drug-store. The prescription I write is a verse from the Bible, Romans 12:2. I do not write out that verse for my patients. I make them look it up and it reads: '. . . be ye transformed by the renewing of your mind . . .' To be happier and healthier they need a renewing of their minds, that is, a change in the pattern of their thoughts. When they 'take' this prescription, they actually achieve a mind full of peace. That helps to produce health and well-being."

A primary method for gaining a quiet mind is to practise emptying the mind. This will be emphasised in another chapter, but I mention it here because it is important. Every day practise emptying the mind of all thoughts that are bothering you: any regrets at your own behaviour, any hurt due to someone else's treatment of you, any failures in your lessons, or feelings of dislike. The mere fact that you consciously make an effort to put these unpleasant memories out of your mind will help you to do so. Haven't you experienced a sense of relief when you have been able to pour out to somebody whom you trust the worries that are troubling you?

I conducted a religious service on board the S.S. "Lurline" on a recent voyage to Honolulu. In the course of my talk I suggested that people with worries go to the stern of the vessel and imaginatively take out each anxious thought, then drop it overboard and watch it disappear in the wake of the ship.

Later on one of the passengers said to me, "I did as you suggested and I am amazed at the relief I feel. During the voyage every evening at sunset I'm going to drop my worries overboard until I get rid of all of them." Doesn't the Bible say something about "forgetting those things which are behind"? Obviously you cannot actually drop a thought overboard, but that concept acts as a symbol of your powerful desire to cast the worry from your mind. The strong wish, as thus expressed, has the tendency to become a fact.

Of course, emptying the mind is not enough. When the mind is emptied, something is bound to enter. The mind cannot long remain a vacuum. You cannot go around permanently with an empty mind. I admit that some people seem to accomplish that feat, but by and large it is necessary to refill the emptied mind or the old, unhappy thoughts which you have cast out will come sneaking in again.

To prevent that happening, immediately start filling your mind with creative and healthy thoughts. Then when the old fears, hates, and worries that have haunted you for so long try to edge back in, they will in effect find a sign on the door of your mind reading "occupied." They may struggle for admission, for having lived in your mind a long time they feel at home there. But the new and healthy thoughts which you have taken in will now be stronger and better fortified, and therefore able to repulse them. Presently the old thoughts will give up altogether and leave you alone. Then you will permanently enjoy a mind full of peace.

At intervals during each day practise thinking a carefully selected series of peaceful thoughts. Let mental pictures of the most peaceful scenes you have ever witnessed pass across your mind as, for example, some beautiful valley filled with the hush of evening time as the shadows lengthen and the sun sinks to rest. Or recall the silvery light of the moon falling upon the rippling waters, or remember the sea washing gently upon soft shores of sand. Such peaceful thought images will work upon your mind as a healing medicine. So now and then during every day allow motion pictures of peace slowly to cross your mind.

Another method for getting a peaceful mind is based on the fact that words have profound suggestive power, and there is healing in the very saying of them. Utter a series of panicky words and your mind will immediately go into a mild state of nervousness. You will perhaps feel butterflies in the pit of your stomach that will affect your entire physical mechanism. If, on the contrary, you speak peaceful, quieting words, your mind will react in a peaceful manner. Use such a word as "tranquillity." Repeat that word slowly several times. "Tranquillity" is one of the most beautiful and melodic of all English words, and the mere saying of it tends to induce a tranquil state.

Another helpful word is "serenity." 'Picturise' serenity as you say it. Repeat it slowly and in the mood of which the word is a symbol. Words such as these have a healing potency when used in this manner.

It is also well to use lines of poetry or passages from the Scriptures. The words of the Bible have a particularly strong ability to heal agitated thoughts. "Drop" them into your mind, allow them to "dissolve" into your consciousness. They will spread healing balm through your entire mental structure. This is one of the simplest processes to perform and also one of the most effective in attaining a quiet mind.

A returned soldier told me of an incident that illustrates this; it happened in Korea where nerves were often raw. One man was so snappy and argumentive that tempers were beginning to flare. Then a quiet GI pulled a small book from his pocket and said, "Bill, I can give you some medicine for those nerves. It will do you good, and I know because it cured me and I was worse off than you are."

The other man snapped at him, but he went on:

"This book will do the job, and I really mean it. I've been carrying this Bible for two years and I don't care who knows it. I've marked places that have helped keep my mind quiet. Want to give it a trial?"

The other grunted, but seeing he was making an impression the GI kept on. "I had an experience one night that started me off. I'd been trying to write home and wasn't getting anywhere with it; I was all keyed up. Then my eye fell on this Bible and I opened it. I read the Twenty-third Psalm which I had learned when I was a young boy. One line hit me: 'He leadeth me beside the still waters; he restoreth my soul.' I kept repeating that over and over. The next thing I knew I woke up. I'd dropped off to sleep holding the pen I'd been trying to write with and the book. I'd only slept about fifteen minutes, but I was rested and refreshed as if I'd had a good night's sleep. I remember it yet, the wonderful feeling I had. Then I realised how peaceful I felt and I kept saying to myself, 'Isn't it strange? What is wrong with me? I've been missing something wonderful.' "

He handed the book to Bill. "Try it," he said. "I'm not nearly so nervous as I used to be. You try it and see."

Bill did try it and got his own tense emotions under control. These two soldiers found that getting a quiet mind isn't complicated. You merely feed your mind with thoughts that cause it to be peaceful. To have a mind full of peace, merely fill it full of peace. It's as simple as that.

There are other practical ways by which you can develop serenity. One way is through your conversation. Depending on the words you use and the tone of voice, you can talk yourself into being nervous and upset. If you want to be peaceful, talk peace. Positive, creative conversation improves situations and helps all concerned.

Suppose you're in a group waiting outside a classroom door.

"Another hour of being bored to death," someone says.

"Wouldn't you think they'd give us teachers who could keep us awake?" agrees another.

But suppose on the other hand one of you says, "I like Old Fuzzy. You have to listen hard but what he says is always important. When I come out of his class I feel that I've learned something."

The others would have followed that lead just as easily. Affirm happy attitudes and your day will be successful and pleasant. So watch your speech if you want a quiet mind. It is important to eliminate from your conversation all negative and upsetting ideas. For example, if you're with a group of friends, don't say glumly, "The Communists will soon take over the country." In the first place, Communists are not going to take over the country; in the second place, by asserting they will do so you create a depressing reaction in the minds of others. Your depressing remark colours their attitudes and everyone goes away with a feeling of annoyance. There are times when we must face these harsh questions and deal with them and no one has more contempt for Communism than I. But as a general thing, to have peace of mind, fill your personal and group conversations with positive, happy, optimistic, satisfying expressions.

The words we speak have a direct and definite effect upon our thoughts. Thoughts create words, for words are the vehicles of ideas. But words also affect thoughts and help to condition if not to create attitudes. In fact, what often passes for thinking starts with talk. Therefore, if the average conversation is scrutinised and disciplined to be sure that it contains peaceful expressions, the result will be peaceful ideas and ultimately a peaceful mind.

Another effective technique in developing a peaceful mind is silence. Especially before exams insist upon not less than a quarter of an hour of absolute quiet every day. Go alone into the quietest place available to you and sit or lie down for fifteen minutes and practise the art of silence. Do not talk to anyone. Do not write. Do not read. Think as little as possible. Throw your mind into neutral. Conceive of your mind as quiescent, inactive. This will not be easy at first because thoughts are stirring up your mind, but practise will increase your efficiency. Picture your mind as the surface of a body of water and see how nearly quiet you can make it, so that there is not a ripple. When you have attained a quiescent state, then begin to listen for the deeper sounds of harmony and beauty and of God that are to be found in the essence of silence.

Perhaps our lack of inner peace is due to some extent to the effect of noise upon the nervous system of modern people. Scientific experiments show that noise in the place where we work, live, or sleep reduces efficiency to a noticeable degree. Contrary to popular belief, it is doubtful if we ever completely adjust our physical, mental or nervous mechanisms to noise. No matter how familiar a repeated sound becomes, it never passes unheard by the subconscious. Automobile horns, the roar of airplanes, and other strident noises actually result in physical activity during sleep. Impulses transmitted to and through the nerves by these sounds cause muscular movements which detract from real rest. If the reaction is sufficiently severe, it partakes of the nature of shock. No wonder so many persons, even young people, are jittery.

In the circumstances of modern life, with its acceleration of pace, the practice of silence is admittedly not so simple as it was in the days of our forefathers. A vast number of noise-producing gadgets exist that they did not know, and our daily programme is more hectic. Space has been annihilated in the modern world, and apparently we are also attempting to annihilate the factor of time. It is only rarely possible for an individual to walk in deep woods or sit by the sea or meditate on a mountaintop or on the deck of a vessel in the midst of the ocean. But when we do have such experiences, we can print on the mind the picture of the silent place and the feel of the moment and return to it in memory to live it over again just as truly as when we were actually in that scene. In fact, when you return to it in memory the mind tends to remove any unpleasant factors present in the actual situation. The memory visit is often an improvement over the actual for the mind tends to reproduce only the beauty in the remembered scene.

Fill your mind with all peaceful experiences possible, then make planned and deliberate excursions to them in memory. You must learn that the easiest way to an easy mind is to create an easy mind. This is done by practice, by the application of some such simple principles as outlined here. The mind quickly responds to teaching and discipline. You can make the mind give you back anything you want, but remember the mind can give back only what it was first given. Saturate your thoughts with peaceful experiences, peaceful words and ideas, and ultimately you will have a storehouse of peace-producing experiences to which you may turn for refreshment and renewal of your spirit. It will be a vast source of power.

I spent a night with a friend who has a very beautiful home. We had breakfast in his unique and interesting dining-room. The four walls are painted in a striking mural picturing the countryside in which my host was reared as a boy. It is a panorama of rolling hills, gentle valleys, and singing streams, the latter clean and sun-speckled, and babbling over rocks. Winding roads meander through pleasant meadows. Little houses dot the landscape. In a central position is a white church surmounted by a tall steeple.

As we breakfasted, my host talked of this region of his youth, pointing out various points of interest in the painting around the wall. Then he said, "Often as I sit in this dining-room I go from point to point in my memory and re-live other days. I recall, for example, walking up that lane as a boy. I remember fishing in that trout stream on many a day in the wintertime.

"There is the church I attended as a boy." He grinned and said, "I sat through many a long sermon in that church but gratefully recall to mind the kindliness of the people and the sincerity of their lives. I can sit here and look at that church and think of the hymns I heard there with my mother and father as we sat together in the pew. They are long buried in that cemetery alongside the church, but in memory I go and stand by their graves and hear them speak to me as in the days gone by. I get very tired and sometimes am nervous and tense. It helps to sit here and go back to the days when I had an untroubled mind, when life was new and fresh. It does something for me. It gives me peace."

Perhaps we all cannot have such murals on our dining-room walls, but you can put them around the wall of your mind—pictures of the most beautiful experiences of your life. Spend time among the thoughts which these pictures suggest. No matter how busy you may be or how hectic your school life becomes, this simple, unique practice, having proved successful in many instances, may have a beneficial effect upon you. It is an easily practised and easy way to a quiet mind.

There is another important factor in this matter of inner peace. If your conscience is tormenting you for some misdeed; if you have lied, cheated, slighted or offended a friend; then you are surely lacking in quietness of spirit. There is a mechanism in each of us that takes over and punishes us. And there is no release except by asking the good Lord to forgive us. He will always bring the release of forgiveness to the spirit of anyone who asks Him and who means it.

Peace of mind is available only by yielding the guilt as well as the tension it produces to the healing therapy of Christ.

At a resort hotel I met a young man whom I had known slightly in New York. He seemed to me extremely nervous, for what reason I couldn't imagine. He came of a well-to-do family. His college grades, I had heard, were satisfactory.

"Doctor," he said suddenly, as we were sitting watching a tennis match, "I would give anything if I could be peaceful and quiet. It's what I want more than anything in this world."

We talked for a bit and it seemed that he was always worrying that something sinister was going to happen, though it never did. His mother, he told me, had always felt that something was going to happen. He had obviously absorbed her fears.

But there was more to his present state than that. His apprehensions were too marked. Was his conscience bothering him? I asked. And that question released a flood of confession. He had a sin on his mind from which he could find no escape. He was the victim of the mechanism of self-punishment.

"Would you like me to pray with you?" I asked hesitantly.

He nodded. So I put my hand on his shoulder and prayed:

"Dear Lord, as You healed people in the long ago and gave them peace, heal this young man now. Give him fully of Thy forgiveness. Help him to forgive himself. Clean the wrong from his mind and let him know that You will not hold it against him. He is sorry for everything. Let Thy peace flow into his mind, into his soul, into his body."

He looked at me with a strange expression on his face; then turned away, for there were tears in his eyes. We were both a bit embarrassed and I left him.

Months later I met him on the street in New York.

He said, "Something happened to me that day you prayed for me. I felt a sense of quietness and peace and healing."

I've seen him frequently since then. He goes to church regularly; reads his Bible; follows the laws of God. He is healthy and happy. And he has a quiet mind and heart.

CHAPTER 3

How to Pray

"EVERY problem can be solved if you pray."

This sentence was quoted to me one day by a young schoolteacher who told me she had had recent proof of the power of prayer. "You've said that often in your books and other writings," she said. "I used it on one of my pupils and I want to tell you that it works."

The story she told me was, I admit, the usual tale of temptation and copying in an examination. Sally, the student, when confronted with it, admitted the fact honestly and without argument. "That," the teacher informed me, "was unexpected since so often, when flat denial fails, the plea is 'everybody does it.' "

But this girl knew what she had done was wrong, admitted that this was not her first offence, and added tearfully—I'm quoting the teacher—that she didn't want to cheat: she wanted to be honest; but at the moment of need she just couldn't help herself.

"So I told her," said the teacher, "she'd really have to learn to pray for strength and also for mental power to do her work well. I prayed with her. For a while we'd meet together and pray every morning before school opened.

"A time came," said the young teacher, her eyes shining with happiness, "when I would see Sally close her eyes during an examination or just before beginning some written assignment. Sally tells me she's not even afraid any more. She knows what to do when she feels tempted."

It is a fact demonstrated so often as to be a sure thing—that every problem can be solved if you pray.

Experts in physical health and well-being, such as coaches, physical education teachers, and health directors, often utilise prayer in their work.

Jack Smith, operator of a health club which is patronised by many outstanding people, believes in the therapy, or physical-conditioning effectiveness, of prayer and uses it. He was at one time a prize fighter, then a truck driver, later a taxi driver, and finally opened his health club. He says that while he probes his patrons for physical flabbiness he also probes for spiritual flabbiness because, he declares, "You can't get a man physically healthy until you get him spiritually healthy."

One day Walter Huston, the actor, sat by Jack Smith's desk. He noted a big sign on the wall on which were penciled the following letters: A P R P B W P R A A. In surprise Huston asked, "What do those letters mean?"

Smith laughed and said, "They stand for: Affirmative Prayers Release Powers By Which Positive Results Are Accomplished."

Huston's jaw dropped in astonishment. "Well, I never expected to hear anything like that in a health club."

"I use methods like that," said Smith, "to make people curious so they will ask what those letters mean. That gives me an opportunity to tell them that I believe affirmative prayers always get results."

Jack Smith, who helps men to keep physically fit, believes that prayer is as important, if not more important, than exercise, steam baths, and a rubdown. It is a vital part of the power-releasing process.

People are doing more praying today than formerly because they find that it adds to personal efficiency. Prayer helps them to tap forces and to utilise strength not otherwise available.

Sir John Hunt, conqueror of Everest, the world's highest mountain, in explaining the important factors that enabled his party to reach the hitherto unattained summit, listed planning, teamwork, excellent equipment. "And," he concluded, "I would add one more asset, intangible, less easy to assess, the thoughts and prayers of all those many who watched and waited for our success. We were aware of this hidden force and we were fortified by it."

And in the final words of his great book, *The Conquest of Everest*,* from which the foregoing

* Cassell & Co. Ltd.

quotation is taken, he concludes with this magnificent statement ". . . there are many other opportunities for adventure . . . there is no height, no depth, that the spirit of man, guided by a higher spirit, cannot attain."

If you have not experienced this power, perhaps you need to learn new techniques of prayer. It is well to study prayer from an efficiency point of view. If you have been praying in a certain manner, even if it has brought you blessings, which it doubtless has, perhaps you can pray even more profitably by varying the pattern and by experimenting with fresh prayer formulas. Get new insights; practise new prayer skills to attain greatest results.

It is important to realise that you are dealing with the most tremendous power in the world when you pray. You would not use an old-fashioned oil lamp for illumination. You want the most up-to-date lighting devices. New and fresh spiritual techniques are being constantly discovered by men and women of spiritual genius. It is advisable to experiment with prayer power according to such methods as prove sound and effective. If this sounds new and strangely scientific, bear in mind that the secret of prayer is to find the process that will most effectively open your mind humbly to God. Any method through which you can stimulate the power of God to flow into your mind is legitimate and usable.

A young man opened a business in New York City a number of years ago, his first establishment being, as he characterised it, "a little hole in the wall." He had one employee. In a few years they moved into a larger room and then into extensive quarters. It became a very successful operation.

This man's method of business, as he described it, was "to fill the little hole in the wall with optimistic prayers and thoughts." He declared that hard work, positive thinking, fair dealing, right treatment of people, and the proper kind of praying always get results. This man, who has a creative and unique mind, worked out his own simple formula for solving his problems and overcoming his difficulties through prayer power. It is a curious formula but I have practised it and personally know that it works. I have suggested it to many people who also found real value in its use. It is recommended to you.

The formula is: (1) PRAYERISE, (2) PICTURISE, (3) ACTUALISE.

By "prayerise" my friend meant a daily system of creative prayer. When a problem arose he talked it over with God very simply and directly in prayer. Moreover, he did not talk with God as to some vast and far-off shadowy being but conceived of God as being with him in his office, in his home, on the street, in his automobile, always near by as a partner, as a close associate. He took seriously the Biblical injunction to "pray without ceasing." He interpreted it as meaning that he should go about every day discussing with God in a natural, normal manner the questions that had to be decided and dealt with. The

Presence came finally to dominate his conscious and ultimately his unconscious thinking. He "prayer-ised" his daily life. He prayed as he walked or drove his car or performed other everyday activities. He filled his daily life full of prayer—that is, he lived by prayer. He did not often kneel to offer his prayers but would, for example, say to God as to a close associate, "What will I do about this, Lord?" or "Give me a fresh insight on this, Lord." He prayerised his mind and so prayerised his activities.

The second point in his formula of creative prayer is to "picturise." The basic factor of physics is force. The basic factor in psychology is the realisable wish. The boy who assumes success tends already to have success. Girls who assume failure tend to have failure. When either failure or success is picturised it strongly tends to actualise in terms equivalent to the mental image pictured.

To assure something worth while happening, first pray about it and test it according to God's will; then print a picture of it on your mind as happening, holding the picture firmly in consciousness. Continue to surrender the picture to God's will—that is to say, put the matter in God's hands—and follow God's guidance. Work hard and intelligently, thus doing your part to achieve success in the matter. Practise believing and continue to hold the picturisation firmly in your thoughts. Do this and you will be astonished at the strange ways in which the picturisation comes to pass. In this manner the picture "actualises." That which you have "prayerised" and "picturised" "actualises" according to the pattern of your basic realisable wish when conditioned by invoking God's power upon it, and if, moreover, you give fully of yourself to its realisation.

For example, a young woman, after five years of married life, discovered that her husband was drifting away from her. He was constantly asking her to have at their house a young girl, newly come to their neighbourhood.

Being a person who prided herself on the direct approach, she accused him of this growing interest. The result was that an unconscious attraction was intensified into a conscious one. The young wife, frightened and bewildered, consulted her minister. He questioned her and discovered that she had been treating her husband with petulance, making scenes, stirring antagonism. Also she had neglected her homemaking, giving him carelessly prepared meals in a messily kept house.

Tactfully he suggested that she build a backfire. He advised her to create in her own mind, and consequently in his, an image of a wife who was always smiling, easy to live with, attractive and charming. Whimsically he told her, "God runs a beauty parlour." Faith and prayer, he told her, could put beauty on a person's face and charm and ease in her manner. He gave her instruction in how to pray and how spiritually to "picturise." He also advised her to hold a mental image of the restoration of the old-time companionship, to visualise the goodness in her husband, and to picture restored harmony between the two of them. She was to hold this picture of faith.

She followed this advice faithfully.

The other girl unwittingly contributed to the wife's strategy by becoming too aggressive. When the day came that her husband complained of this constant intrusion upon their privacy, saying resentfully, "I never seem to have you to myself any more," she knew she had won.

In the grounds of a New England school the night before Commencement, I was walking with a senior who the next evening was to take the leading part in the senior play. Two thousand people would crowd into the gym for this, the biggest event of Commencement Week.

The boy was very nervous and panicky with self-doubt. "How can I ever do it?" he asked.

"Just the way you brought your studies up to good marks, just the way you made the tennis team and forged ahead in other activities," I replied.

"Yes, I know," he said slowly, "by putting myself and what I have to do in God's hands, by trusting God and doing my best—that's what you mean, isn't it?"

"Yes," I replied, "and one more thing: see God with you on that stage tomorrow night, feel His Presence helping you, see yourself as doing the part well and as giving it all you have. See yourself as released and relaxed and able to forget yourself."

The next evening he electrified the crowd. He was wonderful and people commented upon his "inspired" personality.

After the applause had died away and the curtain was rung down he said, as we crossed the old elm-shaded garden that moonlit June night, "I know that God will stick with me if I stick with Him." Then he added, "That technique of visualising God as helping you and picturing yourself as doing all right, that's O.K.; do you know it, very O.K." So commented a young school graduate on the scientific prayer formulas taught in this book.

A young girl, assistant to a playground director in a large city, admitted to her superior that she was haunted by fears for the children. She held her breath, literally, when she saw them crossing the street, even though a policeman might be in charge at that corner and watching out for them. And she was in constant fear of accidents in their often rough play.

The question was put to her gently, asking if she ever prayed.

"Prayer doesn't mean much to me," she confessed.

Then this director talked seriously about the way that prayer, real prayer, could change her: give her confidence instead of fear. If, while she watched the children crossing the street, she would pray, making her prayers an affirmation of God's protective goodness, if she would affirm to herself that she believed in God's love and power to take care of His children, she would find herself losing her fears.

The girl was doubtful, but she agreed to try it. And presently she became an enthusiastic advocate of the success of prayer. She read all the books and pamphlets the director could give her on prayer-power technique.

Another example is that of a very young stenographer who came to me, filled with fear: fear of losing her job, fear of making mistakes that would have serious consequences. I worked with her and outlined the use of prayer as a scientific and practical method for meeting problems. Recently I had the following letter from her.

> I feel I have made wonderful progress in the last few weeks. My greatest progress dates from the night you told me that "every day is a good day if you pray." I began to put into practice the idea of affirming that this would be a good day the minute I woke up in the morning, and *I can positively say that I have not had a bad or upsetting day since that time*. The amazing thing is that my days actually haven't been any smoother or any more free from petty annoyances than they ever were, but they just don't seem to have the power to upset me any more. Every night I begin my prayers by listing all the things for which I am grateful, little things that happened during the day which added to the happiness of my day. I know that this habit has geared my mind to pick out the nice things and forget the unpleasant

ones. The fact that for six weeks I have not had a single bad day and have refused to get down-hearted with anyone is really marvellous to me.

She discovered amazing power in trying prayer power.

You can do the same. Following are ten rules for getting effective results from prayer:

1. Set aside a few minutes every day. Do not say anything. Simply practise thinking about God. This will make your mind spiritually receptive.

2. Then pray orally, using simple, natural words. Tell God anything that is on your mind. Do not think you must use stereotyped pious phrases. Talk to God in your own language. He understands it.

3. Pray as you go about the business of the day. Utilise minute prayers by closing your eyes to shut out the world and concentrating briefly on God's presence. The more you do this every day, the nearer you will feel God's presence.

4. Do not always ask when you pray, but instead affirm that God's blessings are being given, and use most of your prayers to give thanks.

5. Pray with the belief that sincere prayers can reach out and surround your loved ones with God's love and protection.

6. Never use a negative thought in prayer. Only positive thoughts get results.

7. Always express willingness to accept God's will. Ask for what you want, but be willing to take what

God gives you. It may be better than what you ask for.

8. Practise the attitude of putting everything in God's hands. Ask for the ability to do your best and to leave the results confidently to God.

9. Pray for people you do not like or who have mistreated you. Resentment is blockade number one of spiritual power.

10. Make a list of people for whom to pray. The more you pray for other people, especially those not connected with you, the more prayer results will come back to you.

CHAPTER 4

You Make Your Own Happiness

WHO decides whether you shall be happy or unhappy? The answer—you do

A television celebrity had as a guest on his programme an aged man. And he was a very rare old man indeed. His remarks were entirely unpremeditated and of course absolutely unrehearsed. They simply bubbled up out of a personality that was radiant and happy. And whenever he said anything, it was so naïve, so apt, that the audience roared with laughter. They loved him. The celebrity was impressed, and enjoyed it with the others.

Finally he asked the old man why he was so happy. "You must have a wonderful secret of happiness," he suggested.

"No," replied the old man, "I haven't any great secret. It's just as plain as the nose on your face. When I get up in the morning," he explained, "I have two choices—either to be happy or to be unhappy, and what do you think I do? I just choose to be happy, and that's all there is to it."

That may seem an over-simplification, but I recall that Abraham Lincoln said that people were just about as happy as they made up their minds to be. You can be unhappy if you want to be. It is the easiest thing in the world to accomplish. Just choose unhappiness. Go around telling yourself that things aren't going well, that nothing is satisfactory, and you can be quite sure of being unhappy. But say to yourself, "Things are going nicely. Life is good. I choose happiness," and you can be quite certain of having your choice.

Children are more expert in happiness than adults. And the subtlety of Jesus Christ is remarkable, for He tells us that the way to live in this world is to have the childlike heart and mind. So don't become super-sophisticated.

My little daughter Elizabeth, aged eleven, has the answer to happiness. One day I asked her, "Are you happy, honey?"

"Sure I'm happy," she replied.

"Are you always happy?" I asked.

"Sure," she answered, "I'm always happy."

"What makes you happy?" I asked her.

"Why, I don't know," she said, "I'm just happy."

"There must be something that makes you happy," I urged.

"Well," she said, "I'll tell you what it is. My playmates, they make me happy. I like them. My school makes me happy. I like to go to school. I like my teachers. And I like to go to church. I like Sunday school and my Sunday-school teacher. I love my sister Margaret and my brother John. I love my mother and father. They take care of me when I'm sick, and they love me and are good to me."

That is Elizabeth's formula for happiness, and it seems to me that it's all there—her playmates (that's her associates), her school (the place where she works), her church and Sunday school (where she worships), her sister, brother, mother, and father (that means the home circle where love is found). There you have happiness in a nutshell, and the happiest time of your life is in relation to those factors.

A group of boys and girls were asked to list the things that made them happiest. Here is the boys' list: "A swallow flying; looking into deep, clear water; water being cut at the bow of a boat; a fast train rushing; a builder's crane lifting something heavy; my dog's eyes."

And here is what the girls said made them happy: "Street lights on the river; red roofs in the trees; smoke rising from a chimney; red velvet; the moon in the clouds." There is something in the beautiful essence of the universe that is expressed, though only half-articulated, by these things.

Many of us manufacture our own unhappiness. Of course not all unhappiness is self-created, for living conditions are responsible for not a few of our woes. Yet it is a fact that to a large extent by our thoughts and attitudes we distill out of the ingredients of life either happiness or unhappiness for ourselves.

Yet happiness is achievable and the process for obtaining it is not complicated. Anyone who desires it, who wills it, and who learns and applies the right formula may become a happy person.

In a railroad dining car I sat opposite a father and daughter, strangers to me. Obviously the girl was spoiled. Even I, a man not too knowledgeable in such matters, could see that she was very expensively dressed. The fur coat shoved carelessly off her shoulders, the diamond pin at her throat, belonged in my opinion to a much older woman. Her manners were unpleasant: her complaints frequent. She found the dining car draughty, the service "terrible," the food not fit to eat. She said so. I noticed, however, that she ate the food and enjoyed it.

Her father grinned at me. "My daughter," he said, "is in the manufacturing business."

The girl looked across the table at me and decided that I was deserving of an explanation. "My father's being silly," she said. "I don't have to earn my living. My mother left me independently wealthy."

"Nevertheless," said the father cheerfully, "she's in the manufacturing business."

"What does she manufacture?" I asked, willing to play along with him.

"Unhappiness," he replied. "She manufactures her own unhappiness."

Despite the girl's icy indignation, I was grateful for his remark. It describes exactly what most people do—they manufacture their own unhappiness.

It is a pity, too. Life itself provides enough problems to dilute our happiness; it is foolish to add to the difficulties over which we have no control by distilling further unhappiness within our own minds. We manufacture our unhappiness by thinking unhappy thoughts. Perhaps you feel that other people are getting what they do not deserve and you are failing to get what you do deserve. That conviction produces envy, self-pity and consequent misery. How, then, may we proceed to make for ourselves not unhappiness but happiness?

Another incident from one of my railroad journeys may suggest an answer. One morning in an old-style Pullman car approximately a half-dozen of us were shaving in the men's lounge. As always in such close and crowded quarters after a night on the train, this group of strangers was not disposed to be gay, and there was little conversation and that little was mostly mumbled.

Then a man came in wearing on his face a broad smile. He greeted us all with a cheery good morning, but received rather unenthusiastic grunts in return. As he went about his shaving he was humming, probably quite unconsciously, a gay little tune. It got a bit on the nerves of some of the men. Finally one said rather sarcastically, "You certainly seem to be happy this morning! Why all the cheer?"

"Yes," the man answered, "as a matter of fact, I am happy, I do feel cheerful." Then he added. "I make it a habit to be happy."

That is all that was said, but I am sure that each

man in that lounge left the train with those interesting words in mind: "I make it a habit to be happy."

The statement is really very profound, for our happiness or unhappiness depends to an important degree upon the habit of mind we cultivate. That collection of wise sayings, the book of Proverbs, tells us that ". . . he that is of a merry heart hath a continual feast." (Proverbs 15 : 15) In other words, cultivate the merry heart; that is, develop the happiness habit, and life will become a continual feast, which is to say you can enjoy life every day. Out of the happiness habit comes a happy life. And because we can cultivate a habit, we therefore have the power to create our own happiness.

The happiness habit is developed by simply practising happy thinking. Make a mental list of happy thoughts and pass them through your mind several times every day. If an unhappiness thought should enter your mind, immediately stop, consciously eject it, and substitute a happiness thought. Every morning deliberately drop happy thoughts into your conscious mind. Let a series of pictures pass across your mind of each happy experience you expect to have during the day. Savour their joy. Such thoughts will help cause events to turn out that way. Do not affirm that things will not go well that day. By merely saying that, you can actually help to make it so. You will draw to yourself every factor, large and small, that will contribute to unhappy conditions. As a result, you will find yourself asking,

"Why does everything go badly for me? What is the matter with everything?"

The reason can be directly traced to the manner in which you began the day in your thoughts.

Tomorrow try this plan instead. When you get up, say out loud three times this one sentence, "This is the day which the Lord hath made; we will rejoice and be glad in it." (Psalm 118:24) Only personalise it and say, "I will rejoice and be glad in it." Repeat it in a strong, clear voice and with positive tone and emphasis. The statement, of course, is from the Bible and it is a good cure for unhappiness. If you repeat that one sentence three times before breakfast and meditate on the meaning of the words you will change the character of the day by starting off with a happiness psychology.

While dressing, say aloud a few such remarks as the following: "I believe this is going to be a wonderful day. I believe I can successfully handle all problems that will arise today. I feel good physically, mentally, emotionally. It is wonderful to be alive. I am grateful for all that I have had, for all that I now have, and for all that I shall have. Things aren't going to fall apart. God is here and He is with me and He will see me through. I thank God for every good thing."

I once knew a young fellow who always said to his parents at breakfast, "This is going to be another tough day at school." He didn't really think so, but he had a mental quirk whereby if he said it was going to be a tough day, it might turn out pretty well. But things really started going badly with him in his studies and athletically—he had hoped to make the football eleven. This was not surprising, for if you visualise and affirm an unhappy outcome, you tend thereby to create just that type of condition. So affirm happy outcomes at the start of every day, and you will be surprised at how often thing will turn out so. The boy just mentioned eventually got on to this method of happy and positive affirmation and is doing very well indeed.

But it is not sufficient to apply to the mind what I have just suggested; throughout the day you must base your actions and attitudes upon fundamental principles of happy living.

One of the most simple and basic of such principles is that of human service and goodwill. It is amazing what happiness a sincere expression of compassion and friendly helpfulness will induce.

My friend Dr. Samuel Shoemaker once wrote a moving story about a mutual friend, Ralston Young, famous as Redcap No. 42 in the Grand Central Station in New York. Ralston carries bags for a living, but his real job is living the spirit of Christ as a redcap in one of the world's greatest railway stations. As he carries a man's suitcase, he tries to share a little Christian fellowship with him. He carefully watches a customer to see if there is any way in which he can give him more courage and hope. He is very skilful in the way he goes about it, too.

One day, for example, he was asked to take a little old lady to her train. She was in a wheel-chair, so he took her down on the elevator. As he wheeled her into the elevator he noticed that there were tears in her eyes. Ralston Young stood there as the elevator descended, closed his eyes, and asked the Lord how he could help her, and the Lord gave him an idea. As he wheeled her off the elevator, he said with a smile, "Ma'am, if you don't mind my saying so, that is a mighty pretty hat you are wearing."

She looked up at him and said, "Thank you."

"And I might add," he said, "that sure is a pretty dress you have on. I like it so much."

Being a woman, this appealed to her, and despite the fact that she was not feeling well, she brightened up and asked, "Why in the world did you say those nice things to me? It was very thoughtful of you."

"Well," he said, "I saw how unhappy you were. I saw that you were crying, and I just asked the Lord how I could help you. The Lord said, 'Speak to her about her hat.' The mention of the dress," he added, "was my own idea." Ralston Young and the Lord together knew how to get a woman's mind off her troubles.

"Don't you feel well?" he then asked.

"No," she replied. "I am constantly in pain. I am never free from it. Sometimes I think I can't stand it. Do you, by any chance, know what it means to be in pain all the time?"

Ralston had an answer. "Yes, ma'am, I do, for I

lost an eye, and it hurts like a hot iron day and night."

"But," she said, "you seem to be happy now. How did you accomplish it?"

By this time he had her in her seat in the train, and he said, "Just by prayer, ma'am, just by prayer."

Softly she asked, "Does prayer, just prayer, take your pain away?"

"Well," answered Ralston, "perhaps it doesn't always take it away. I can't say that it does, but it always helps to overcome it so it doesn't seem like it hurts so much. Just keep on prayin', ma'am, and I'll pray for you too."

Her tears were dried now, and she looked up at him with a lovely smile, took him by the hand, and said, "You've done me so much good "

A year passed, and one night in Grand Central Station Ralston Young was paged to come to the information booth. A young woman was there who said, "I bring you a message from the dead. Before she died my mother told me to find you and to tell you how much you helped her last year when you took her to the train in her wheel-chair. She will always remember you, even in eternity. She will remember you, for you were so kind and loving and understanding." Then the young woman burst into tears and sobbed in her grief.

Ralston stood quietly watching her. Then he said, "Don't cry, missy, don't cry. You shouldn't cry. Give a prayer of thanksgiving."

Surprised, the girl said, "Why should I give a prayer of thanksgiving?"

"Because," said Ralston, "many people have become orphans much younger than you. You had your mother for a long, long time, and besides you still have her. You will see her again. She is near to you now and she always will be near to you. Maybe," he said, "she is right with us now—the two of us, as we talk."

The sobs ended and the tears dried. Ralston's kindness had the same effect on the daughter as it had had on the mother. In this huge station, with thousands of people passing by, the two of them felt the presence of One who inspired this wonderful redcap to go around this way spreading love and helping to take people's pain away.

"Where love is," said Tolstoy, "God is," and, we might add, where God and love are, there is happiness. So a practical principle in creating happiness is to practise love.

I have a friend who is a genuinely happy man. He travels throughout the country in his work and carries a unique business card. On one side is his name and address and on the reverse it states his philosophy which has brought happiness not only to him but to hundreds of other people. It reads as follows: "The way to happiness: keep your heart free from hate, your mind from worry. Expect little, give much. Forget self, think of others."

As you read these words you may say, "There's

nothing new in that." Indeed, there is something new in it if you've never tried it. Start to practise it and you will find it the newest, freshest, most astonishing method of happy and successful living you have ever used. Perhaps you have known these principles all your life. But what is their value to you if you've never made use of them? You've been living in poverty when you had this gold on your doorstep.

Practise these principles and you will find they will bring you real happiness. Keep your heart free from hate: that is, don't let yourself dislike anybody —not the boy across the aisle who is always showing off and getting into trouble, not the teacher who blames you for what you didn't do. Stand up for yourself, straighten out the difficulty, but don't brood over it. Don't worry about it. Hate the deed, but not the person. Never dislike anybody; that is, if you want to be happy.

Expect little, give much. That's not easy. When we give, we expect at least an equal return. But if we make a habit of giving more than we get, we'll find ourselves enjoying life more. It really works out that way. Don't think about getting your mother to do something for you: think about what you can do for her. And don't do this today only: keep at it, today and tomorrow and tomorrow. It's when you have made a habit of practising the behaviour that brings happiness that you will find yourself continuously happy.

In my travels about the country I have been encountering an increasing number of genuinely happy individuals of all ages. These are persons who have been practising the techniques described in this book, and which I have presented in other volumes and in other writings and talks, and which other writers and speakers have likewise been giving to receptive people.

It is astonishing how people can become inoculated with happiness through an inner experience of spiritual change. People of all types everywhere are having this experience today. In fact, it has become one of the most popular happenings of our times, and if it continues to develop and expand, the person who has not had a real spiritual experience will soon be considered old-fashioned and behind the times. Nowadays it is smart to be spiritually alive. It is stuffed-shirtism to be ignorant of that happiness-producing transformation which people everywhere are enjoying at this time.

Recently, after I had finished a lecture in a certain city, a big, fine-looking young man came up to me. He slapped me on the shoulder with such force that it almost bowled me over.

"Doctor," he said in a booming voice, "how about coming out with the gang? We are having a big party at the Smiths' house, and we would like you to come along. It's going to be a whale of a shindig and you ought to get in on it." So ran his racy invitation.

Well, obviously this didn't sound like a proper party for a preacher, and I was hesitant. I was afraid I might cramp everyone's style, so I began to make excuses.

"Oh, forget it," my friend told me. "Don't worry, this is your kind of party. You will be surprised. Come on along. You will get the kick of your life out of it."

So I yielded and went along with my buoyant and racy friend and he was certainly one of the most infectious personalities I had encountered in quite a while. Soon we came to a big house set back among trees with a wide, sweeping driveway up to the front door. Judging by the noise issuing from the open windows there was no question that quite a party was in progress, and I wondered what I was getting into. My host, with a great shout, dragged me into the room, and we had quite a handshaking time; he introduced me to a large group of gay and exhuberant people. They were a happy, joyous lot of young folk.

I looked around for a bar, but there wasn't any. All that was being served was coffee, fruit juice, ginger ale, sandwiches, and ice cream, but there was lots of those.

"These people must have stopped somewhere before coming here," I remarked to my friend.

He was shocked, and said, "Stopped somewhere? Why, you don't understand. These people have the spirit all right, but not the kind of 'spirit' you are thinking about. I am surprised at you," he said. "Don't you realise what makes this gang so happy? They have got something. They have been set free from themselves. They have found God as a living, vital, honest-to-goodness reality. Yes," he said, "they have got spirit all right, but it isn't the kind that you get out of a bottle. They have got spirit in their hearts."

Then I saw what he meant. This wasn't a crowd of sad-faced, stodgy people. They were the leaders of the young crowd of that town, and they were having a wonderful time at this party—talking about God, and they were doing it in the most natural manner imaginable. They were telling one another about the changes that had occurred in their lives through revitalised spiritual power.

Those who have the naïve notion that you can't laugh and be gay when you are religious should have attended that party.

Well, I went away with a Bible verse running through my mind, "In him was life; and the life was the light of men." (John 1 : 4) That was the light I saw on the faces of those happy people. An inner light was reflected outwardly on their faces, and it came from an effervescent spiritual something that they had taken into themselves. Life means vitality, and these people obviously were getting their vitality from God. They had found the power that creates happiness.

This is no isolated incident. I venture the assertion that in your own community, if you will look around for them, you will find lots of people—many of them young like yourselves—similar to those described above. If you don't find them in your own home town, come to the Marble Collegiate Church in New York City and you will find them by the score. But you can get the same spirit by reading this book if you practise the simple principles set forth.

As you read this book, believe what you read, because it is true; then start working on the practical suggestions the book contains and you, too, will have the spiritual experience that produces this quality of happiness. Thus, having been changed inwardly, you will begin to create out of yourself not unhappiness, but a happiness of such quality and character that you will wonder if you are living in the same world. As a matter of fact it won't be the same world because you are not the same, and what you are determines the world in which you live; so as you change, your world changes also.

This is the secret of happiness. All else is secondary. Get this experience and you've got real, unalloyed happiness, the best the world offers. Don't miss it whatever you do in this life, for this is it.

CHAPTER 5

Stop Fuming and Fretting

ARE you a boy or girl who fumes and frets? The word "fume" means to boil up, to blow off, to seethe. The word "fret" is equally descriptive. It has an irritating, annoying, penetrating quality. It is a childish term, reminding you of a fretful baby. The Bible says, "Fret not thyself . . ." (Psalm 37 : 1) That is sound advice for the people of our time, young and old. We need to stop fuming and fretting; we need to become peaceful if we are to have power to live effectively.

The character of our thoughts determines the pace at which we live. When the mind goes rushing pell-mell from one feverish idea to another, we become irritable and impatient. This mood produces toxic poisons in the body and creates a sort of emotional illness. We feel frustrated and fume and fret about everything. Such emotional disquiet affects us physically; it even reaches that deeper inner essence of the personality known as the soul.

It is impossible to have peace of soul if you live at so feverishly accelerated a pace. God won't go that fast. He will not endeavour to keep up with you.

He says in effect, "Go ahead if you like. When you are worn out, ask for My healing. I can make your life so rich that you will be glad to slow down. Then you will learn to live and move and have your being in Me."

God moves deliberately and with perfect timing. The only wise rate at which to live is at God's rate. God gets things done, and they are done right. He does them without hurry. He neither fumes nor frets. He is peaceful: and therefore efficient. And He offers us this same peace: "Peace I leave with you, My peace I give unto you . . ." (John 14:27)

One wonders whether this generation is not so accustomed to tension that many are in the unhappy state of not being comfortable without it. The deep quietness of woods and valleys so well known to our forefathers is an unaccustomed state to them. The tempo of their lives is such that in many instances they have an incapacity to draw upon the sources of peace and quietness which the physical world offers.

One summer afternoon my wife and I went for a long walk in the woods. We were stopping at the beautiful Lake Mohonk Mountain House, which is set in one of the finest natural parks in America, 7,500 acres of virgin mountainside in the middle of which is a lake lying like a gem in the forest. The word *mohonk* means "lake in the sky." Aeons ago some giant upheaval of the earth cast up these sheer cliffs. You come out of the deep woods on to some noble promontory and there before you are great valleys set among hills, rock-ribbed and ancient as the sun. These woods, mountains, and valleys constitute what ought to be a sure retreat from every confusion of this world.

On this afternoon as we walked there was a mixture of summer showers and sunlit hours. We were drenched and started to fret about it a bit because it took the press out of our clothes. Then we told each other that it doesn't hurt a human being to get drenched with clean rain water, that the rain feels cool and fresh on one's face, and that you can always sit in the sun and dry yourself out. We walked under the trees and talked and then fell silent.

We were listening, listening deeply to the quietness. In a strict sense, the woods are never still. There is tremendous activity always in process, but nature makes no strident noises regardless of the vastness of its operation. Nature's sounds are quiet, harmonious.

On this beautiful afternoon, nature was laying its hand of healing quietness upon us, and we could actually feel the tension being drawn off.

Just as we were falling under this spell, the faint sounds of what passes for music came to us. It was nervous, high-strung music of the jitterbug variety. Presently through the woods came three young people, two girls and a young man, and the latter was lugging a portable radio.

They were three young city people out for a walk

in the woods and tragically enough were bringing their noise along with them. They were nice young folk, too, for they stopped and we had a pleasant talk with them. It occurred to me to ask them to turn that thing off and listen to the music of the woods, but I didn't feel it was my business to instruct them, and finally they went on their way.

We commented on the loss they were incurring, that they could pass through this peacefulness and not give ear to the music that is as old as the world, harmony and melody the like of which man has never equalled: the song of the wind through the trees, the sweet notes of birds singing their hearts out, the whole background of the music of the spheres.

This is still to be found in our woods and great plains, in our valleys, in our mountain majesties, and where the ocean foams on soft shores of sand. We should avail ourselves of its healing. Remember the words of Jesus, "Come ye yourselves apart into a desert place, and rest a while." (Mark 6:21) Even as I write these words and give you this good advice, I recall instances where it has been necessary to remind myself to practise the same truth, which emphasises that we must everlastingly discipline ourselves to quietness if we expect its benefits in our lives.

One autumn day Mrs. Peale and I took a trip into Massachusetts to see our son John at Deerfield Academy. We told him we would arrive at 11 a.m.

and we pride ourselves on the good old-fashioned custom of promptness. Therefore, being a bit behind schedule, we were driving at breakneck speed through the autumnal landscape. My wife said, "Norman, did you see that radiant hillside?"

"What hillside?" I asked.

"It just went by on the other side," she explained. "Look at that beautiful tree."

"What tree?" I was already a mile past it.

"This is one of the most glorious days I have ever seen," my wife said. "How could you possibly imagine such amazing colours as these New England hillsides in October? In fact," she said, "it makes me happy inside."

That remark of hers so impressed me that I stopped the car and went back a quarter of a mile to a lake backed by towering hills dressed in autumn colours. We sat and looked and meditated. God with His genius and skill had painted that scene in the varied colours which He alone can mix. In the still waters of the lake lay a reflected vision of His glory, for the hillside was unforgettably pictured in that mirror-like pond.

For quite a while we sat without a word until finally my wife broke the silence by the only appropriate statement that one could make, "He leadeth me beside the still waters." (Psalm 23:2) We arrived at Deerfield at eleven, but we were not tired. In fact, we were deeply refreshed.

To help reduce this tension which seems to dominate our people of all ages everywhere, you can start by reducing your own pace. To do that you will need to slow down, quiet down. Do not fume. Do not fret. Practise being relaxed. Practise "the peace of God which passeth all understanding." (Phillippians 4:7) Then note the quiet power sense that swells up within you.

A teacher was talking with one of his more promising students about the courses he must take the following year in order to meet college entrance requirements. "Of course you're planning on going to college, aren't you, Ned?" he said.

"I don't know," answered the boy. "I can't get my father to say."

"Why can't you?" The teacher was puzzled. He knew the boy's father, a manufacturer, well and had always found him reasonable and approachable.

"He's so busy and tense: he comes home with such a lot of work to do. After supper he shuts himself up and works until after I've gone to bed. I just don't have a chance to talk to him. Besides he's so nervous it is hard to get him in the right mood."

"Mm." The teacher thought for a moment. "I'll talk to him," he decided. "Maybe your mother would ask me to go home to dinner with you after church next Sunday. Think she would?"

The boy grinned. "She'll ask you," he promised.

The dinner table conversation that following Sunday was as easy and pleasant as had been all that teacher's contacts with this family.

"What about a walk?" he suggested to the father as they were leaving the table.

The other man consented courteously. And the visiting teacher—we'll call him Rodney Stone—guided their walk to the town's very beautifully kept cemetery. "This place is so near your office: I suppose you come here often?" he suggested to his friend.

"When would I have time to do that? And besides it doesn't make sense," the other answered impatiently. "Man! I have a job that works me ten hours a day and two or three extra hours every night! Come walking in a cemetery! Why would I do that?"

"Because you need it, Edward," said the other grimly. "If ever I saw a man heading for a nervous breakdown, you're the man."

"I know," admitted the other.

"Why do you take work home?" asked Stone. "You employ some very capable young men. Make one of them do it."

"I'm the only one that can attend to these matters," said the other testily. "There isn't time to let someone else make mistakes. My work has to be done quickly. Everything depends on me. Do you want to see my business go on the rocks?"

"No," agreed his friend. "Nor do I want to see you go on the rocks where you're heading. Sit down, Ed."

They did sit down: on one of the tombstones.

And there was something about the quietude of the place that soothed the taut nerves of the manufacturer.

"You and I are going to be here permanently one of these days," said the teacher. And he added: "I suppose the world will go on just the same. Even the work you are doing will go on: your factory won't shut down except for a day or so out of respect for your passing." He quoted the fourth verse of the 90th Psalm: ". . . a thousand years in Thy sight are but as yesterday when it is past, and as a watch in the night."

The next day after school the boy came to this teacher's desk. "Don't know what you did to Dad," he grinned, "but he came home a changed man. He was so relaxed that we had a nice talk. It's settled: about college, I mean. I'm to go."

I could tell you any number of such stories about how tense present-day people get and how it affects young people too. Before you know it, they too are high-strung like an over-tight violin string. Start now, early in life, to practise the great art of easy-does-itness. Learn to keep calm.

A friend of mine, a prominent young business man, was so eager to get ahead that he got to doing what baseball men call over-pressing. He had formed the habit of driving himself at such speed that, as he described it to me, he leapt out of bed every morning and immediately got himself into high gear. He was in such a rush and a dither that he said,

"I eat soft-boiled eggs for breakfast because they slide down fast." This hectic pace left him fagged and worn at about midday. He sank into bed every night exhausted.

It so happens that his home is situated in a grove of trees. Very early one morning, unable to sleep, he arose and sat by the window. He became interested in watching a bird emerge from his night's sleep. He noticed that a bird sleeps with his head under his wing, the feathers pulled all around himself. When he awakened, he pulled his bill out from under his feathers, took a sleepy look around, stretched one leg to its full length, meanwhile stretching the wing over the leg until it spread out life a fan. He pulled the leg and wing back, and then repeated the same process with the other leg and wing, whereupon he put his head down in his feathers again for a delicious little cat nap (only in this case a bird nap), then the head came out again. This time the bird looked around eagerly, threw his head back, gave his wings and legs two more big stretches, then he sent up a song, a thrilling, melodic song of praise to the day, wherewith he hopped down off the limb, got himself a drink of cold water, and started looking for food.

My highly-strung friend said to himself, "If that's the way the birds get up, sort of slow and easy like, why wouldn't it be a good method for me to start the day that way?" He actually went through the same performance, even to singing, and noticed that the song was an especially beneficial factor, that it was a releasing mechanism.

"I can't sing," he chuckled, "but I practised sitting quietly in a chair and singing. Mostly I sang hymns and happy songs. Imagine me singing, but I did. My wife thought I was bereft of my senses. The only thing I had on the bird was that I did a little praying, too; then, like the bird, I felt like some food, and I wanted a good breakfast—bacon and eggs. And I took my time eating it. After that I went to work in a released frame of mind. It surely did start me off for the day minus the tension, and it helped me go through the day in a peaceful and relaxed manner."

A member of a championship university crew told me that their shrewd crew coach often reminded them, "To win this or any race, row slowly." He pointed out that rapid rowing tends to break the stroke and when the stroke is broken it is with the greatest difficulty that a crew recovers the rhythm necessary to win. Meanwhile other crews pass the disorganised group. It is indeed wise advice—"To go fast, row slowly."

In order to row slowly or to work slowly and maintain the steady pace that wins, the victim of high tempo will do well to get the co-ordinating peace of God into his mind, his soul, and, it might be added, into his nerves and muscles also.

Have you ever considered the importance of having the peace of God in your muscles, in your joints?

Your muscles will work with correlation when the peace of God who created them governs their action. Speak to your muscles every day and to your joints and to your nerves, saying, "Fret not thyself." In due course your muscles and joints will take heed.

Slow down, for whatever you really want will be there when you get there if you work toward it without stress, without pressing. If, proceeding under God's guidance and in His smooth and unhurried tempo, you find it is not there, then it is not supposed to be there. If you miss it, perhaps you should have missed it. So definitely seek to develop a normal, natural, God-ordered pace. Practise and preserve mental quiet. Learn the art of letting go all nervous excitement. To do this, stop at intervals and affirm, "I now relinquish nervous excitement—it is flowing from me. I am at peace." Do not fume. Do not fret. Practise being peaceful.

To attain this efficient state of living, I recommend the practice of thinking peaceful thoughts. Every day we perform a series of acts designed to care for the body properly. We bathe, brush the teeth, take exercise. In similar fashion we should give time and planned effort to keeping the mind in a healthy state. One way to do this is to sit quietly and pass a series of peaceful thoughts through the mind. For example, pass through the thoughts the memory of a lofty mountain, a misty valley, a sun-speckled trout stream, silver moonlight on water.

At least once in every twenty-four hours deliberately stop whatever you are doing for ten or fifteen minutes and practise serenity.

There are times when it is essential resolutely to check our headlong pace, and it must be emphasised that the only way to stop is to stop.

I went to a certain city on a lecture date and was met at the train by a committee. I was rushed to a bookstore where I had an autographing party and then to another bookstore where another autographing party was held. Then they rushed me to a luncheon. After rushing through the luncheon I was rushed to a meeting. After the meeting I was rushed back to the hotel where I changed my clothes and was rushed to a reception where I met several hundred people and drank three glasses of fruit punch. Then I was rushed back to the hotel and told I had twenty minutes to dress for dinner. When I was getting dressed the telephone rang and somebody said, "Hurry, hurry, we must rush down to dinner."

Excitedly I chattered, "I will rush right down."

I rushed from the room and was so excited that I could scarcely get the key into the lock. Hastily I felt myself, to be sure that I was completely dressed, and rushed toward the elevator. All of a sudden I stopped. I was out of breath. I asked myself, "What is this all about? What is the meaning of this ceaseless rush? This is ridiculous!"

Then I declared independence, and said, "I do not care if I go to dinner. I do not care whether I give a talk. I do not have to go to this dinner and

I do not have to make a speech." So deliberately and slowly I walked back to my room and took my time about unlocking the door. I telephoned the man downstairs and said, "If you want to eat, go ahead. If you want to save a place for me, I will be down after a while, but I am not going to rush any more."

So I removed my coat, sat down, took off my shoes, put my feet up on the table, and just sat. Then I opened the Bible and very slowly read aloud the 121st Psalm, "I will lift up mine eyes unto the hills, from whence cometh my help." I closed the book and had a little talk with myself, saying, "Come on now, start living a slower and more relaxed life," and then I affirmed, "God is here and His peace is touching me.

"I do not need anything to eat," I reasoned. "I eat too much anyway. Besides, the dinner will probably not be very good, and if I am quiet now I will give a better speech at eight o'clock."

So I sat there resting and praying for fifteen minutes. I shall never forget the sense of peace and personal mastery I had when I walked out of that room. I had the glorious feeling of having overcome something, of having taken control of myself emotionally, and when I reached the dining-room the others had just finished the first course. All I missed was the soup, which by general consent was no great loss.

This incident was an amazing experience of the healing presence of God. I gained these values by simply stopping, by quietly reading the Bible, by sincerely praying, and by thinking some peaceful thoughts for a few moments.

Physicians generally seem to feel that many physical troubles could be avoided by *not* fuming and fretting. One young man in his late twenties came to me at his doctor's suggestion.

"He says I'm too tense and highly strung," said the man, rising to pace the floor. "He says I must develop what he calls a calm philosophy of living. How in the world can I do that? It's a lot easier said than done."

That did indeed seem to be a problem for he was a bundle of excitable and explosive nerves. He paced the floor, thumped the table, his voice was high-pitched.

As I listened to him and watched him I again understood why Jesus Christ retains his remarkable hold on men. It is because he has the answer to such problems as this.

I proved that fact by suddenly changing the line of the conversation. Without any introductory words I began to recite certain Bible texts such as: "Come unto me . . . and I will give you rest." (Matthew 11:28) "Peace I leave with you, my peace I give unto you. . . . Let not your heart be troubled." (John 14:27) And still another: "Thou wilt keep him in perfect peace, whose mind is stayed on Thee." (Isaiah 26:3)

I recited these words slowly, deliberately, reflectively. As this reciting went on, I noticed that my visitor stopped being agitated. Quietness came over him and then we both sat in silence. It seemed that we sat so for several minutes. Perhaps it wasn't that long, but finally he took a deep breath.

"Why, that's funny," he said. "I feel a lot better. Isn't that queer? I guess it was those words that did it."

"No, not the words alone," I answered, "though they do have a remarkable effect upon the mind, but something deeper happened just then. He touched you a minute ago—the Physician with the healing touch. He was present in this room."

My visitor evinced no surprise at this assertion, but eagerly and impetuously agreed—conviction was written on his face. "That's right, He sure was. I felt Him. I see what you mean. Now I understand—Jesus Christ will help me develop a calm philosophy of living."

This man found what increasing thousands are discovering, that a simple faith in and practice of the principles and techniques of Christianity bring peace and quietness and therefore new power to body, mind, and spirit. It is the perfect antidote to fuming and to fretting. It helps a person to become peaceful and thus to tap new resources of strength.

In attaining emotional control the daily practice of healing techniques is of first importance. Emotional control cannot be gained in any magical or easy way. You cannot develop it by merely reading a book, although that is often helpful. The only sure method is by working at it regularly, persistently, scientifically, and by developing creative faith.

I suggest that you begin with such a primary procedure as the practice of keeping physically still. Don't pace the floor. Don't wring your hands. Don't let yourself get worked up into a dither. In excitement one's physical movements became accentuated. Therefore begin at the simplest place, that is by ceasing physical movement. Stand still, sit down, lie down. Certainly keep the voice down to a low pitch.

In developing a calm control it is necessary to think calmness, for the body responds sensitively to the type of thoughts that pass through the mind. It is also true that the mind can be quieted by first making the body quiet. That is to say, a physical attitude can induce desired mental attitudes.

I was at a meeting where a discussion was going on which finally became rather bitter. Tempers were becoming frayed and some of the participants were decidedly on edge. Sharp remarks were passed. Suddenly one man arose, deliberately took off his coat, opened his collar, and lay down upon a couch. All were astonished, and someone asked if he felt ill.

"No," he said, "I feel fine, but I am beginning to get angry, and I have learned that it is difficult to get angry lying down."

We all laughed, and the tension was broken. Then our whimsical friend went on to explain that he had "tried a little trick" with himself. He had a quick temper, and when he felt himself getting angry he found that he was clenching his fist and raising his voice, so he deliberately extended his fingers, not allowing them to form into a fist. In proportion to the rising of his tension or anger, he depressed his voice and talked in exaggerated low tones. "You cannot carry on an argument in a whisper," he said with a grin.

This principle can be effective in controlling emotional excitements, fretting, as many have discovered by experimentation. A beginning step, therefore, in achieving calmness is to discipline your physical reactions. You will be surprised at how quickly this can reduce the heat of your emotions; and when emotional heat is driven off, fuming and fretting subside. You will be amazed at the energy and power you will save. You will be much less tired.

It is, moreover, a good procedure to practise being phlegmatic or apathetic, even indifferent. To a certain extent even practise being sluggish. People thus constituted are less likely to emotional breaks. Highly organised individuals may do well to cultivate these reactions to a degree at least.

Naturally one does not want to lose the keen, sensitive responsiveness characteristic of the highly organised individual. But the practice of being phlegmatic tends to bring such a keyed-up personality to a balanced emotional position.

I am listing here five points which I, personally,

have found helpful in reducing the tendency to fume and fret.

1. Sit, stand, or walk in an exceedingly relaxed manner.

2. Spend two or three minutes thinking of the most beautiful and peaceful scenes you can remember: a mountain at sunset, a valley white with the mists of early morning, the quiet of the woods at noonday, moonlight on rippling waters. In memory relive these scenes.

3. Repeat slowly, bringing out the melody of each, such words as (*a*) tranquillity; (*b*) serenity; (*c*) quietness. Or repeat some poem you have memorised that carries the mood of peace and quiet.

4. Remember and dwell on the times when you have been conscious of God's watchful care. Recall times when you were worried or anxious and turned to Him for help, and He brought you through. Recite a line from some old hymn, such as "So long Thy power hath kept me, sure it STILL will lead me on."

5. Repeat the following, which has an amazing power to relax and quiet the mind: "Thou wilt keep him in perfect peace, whose mind is stayed on Thee." Repeat this during the day, whenever you have a fraction of a moment or feel in need of its reassuring quietude. Repeat it aloud when possible.

As you work with the technique suggested in this chapter, the tendency to fume and fret will gradually be modified. In direct proportion to your progress, the power formerly drawn off and wasted by this unhappy habit will be felt in your increased ability to meet the events of your life. Learn to live the calm and easy way; no stress; no dither. As you swing a bat "easy like" for easy power, get in harmony with God and have easy power in your life.

CHAPTER 6

You Get What You Expect

"It's useless to send my boy to college," a troubled father said to me. "He's had to carry five subjects all the way through high school: four advanced, and one make-up. He seems to have a genius for failure. I'm greatly disturbed about his future."

I tried to reassure the man, telling him of other boys I knew who, as they grew older, got on to themselves, so to speak, and learned the curiously simple but potent answer of turning failure into success. And this proved true in the case of this boy: he did acquire the secret. His personality began to focus, his powers to fuse. He went through college very well indeed. He became a leader in school activities, and his marks were well up. After graduation he got a good job and while still in his twenties was a prominent person in town.

Not long ago at a luncheon I could not help admiring the dynamic young man who presided—the boy whose father had said he had a genius for failure. He had, I knew, worked up an original idea into a coming business and was already a leader in his community. I asked him about the reasons for his success.

"It is quite simple," he replied. "I merely learned the magic of believing. If you expect the worst, you get the worst. If you expect the best, you will get the best. If you think right, things will go right. It all comes of practising a verse from the Bible."

"And what is that verse?" I asked.

He smiled at me and his smile was charming. "You ought to know," he said. "You gave it to me. You emphasised it in a talk I heard you give one Sunday when I attended your church. 'If thou canst believe, all things are possible to him that believeth.'" (Mark 9:23)

That, in essence, is the simple answer which anyone—boy or man, girl or woman—can follow who is trying to turn failure into success. Train your mind to believe, to think positively, to have faith in God and yourself. Expect the best and you will get the best. It sounds miraculous, but it isn't at all. Think and live this way and you are using one of the most powerful laws in this world, a law recognised alike by psychology and religion; namely, change your mental habits to belief instead of disbelief. Learn to expect, not to doubt. In so doing you bring everything into the realm of possibility.

This does not mean that simply by believing or by positive thinking you are going to get everything you want or think you want. But it does definitely mean that when you learn to believe and think with creative positiveness, that which has seemingly been impossible moves into the area of the possible. Every great thing at last becomes for you a possibility. Indeed, when you put your trust in God, He guides your mind so that you do not want things that are not good for you or that are inharmonious with His will.

So, to learn to believe is of primary importance. It is the basic factor of succeeding in any undertaking. When you expect the best, you release a magnetic force in your mind which by a law of attraction tends to bring the best to you. But if you expect the worst, you release from your mind the power of repulsion which tends to force the best from you. It is amazing how a sustained expectation of the best sets in motion forces which cause the best to materialise.

As a boy, living in the Midwest, my favourite writer of sport stories was a then popular writer, Hugh Fullerton. One story which I have never forgotten concerned Josh O'Reilly, one time manager of the San Antonio Club of the Texas league. O'Reilly had a roster of great players, seven of whom had been hitting over three hundred, and everybody thought his team would easily take the championship. But the club fell into a slump and lost seventeen of the first twenty games. The players simply couldn't hit anything, and each began to accuse the other of being a "jinx" to the team.

Playing the Dallas Club, a rather poor team that year, only one San Antonia player got a hit, and that, strangely enough, was the pitcher. O'Reilly's team was badly beaten that day. In the clubhouse after the game, the players were a disconsolate lot. Josh O'Reilly knew that he had an aggregation of stars and he realised that their trouble was simply that they were thinking wrongly. They didn't expect to get a hit. They didn't expect to win. They expected to be defeated. They were thinking not victory but defeat. Their mental pattern was not one of expectation but of doubt. This negative mental process inhibited them, froze their muscles, threw them off their timing, and there was no free flow of easy power through the team.

It so happened that a preacher named Schlater was popular in that neighbourhood at that time. He claimed to be a faith healer and apparently was getting some astounding results. Throngs crowded to hear him and almost everybody had confidence in him. Perhaps the fact that they did believe in his power enabled Schlater to achieve results.

O'Reilly asked each player to lend him his two best bats. Then he asked the members of the team to stay in the clubhouse until he returned. He put the bats in a wheelbarrow and went off with them. He was gone for an hour. He returned jubilantly to tell the players that Schlater, the preacher, had blessed the bats and that these bats now contained a power that could not be overcome. The players were astounded and delighted.

The next day they overwhelmed Dallas, getting thirty-seven base hits and twenty runs. They hammered their way through the league to a championship, and Hugh Fullerton said that for years in the Southwest a player would pay a large sum for a "Schlater bat."

Regardless of the question of Schlater's personal power, the fact remains that something tremendous happened in the minds of those ball players. Their thought pattern was changed. They began thinking in terms of expectation, not doubt. They expected not the worst, but the best. They expected hits, runs, victories, and they got them. They had the power to get what they wanted. There was no difference in the bats themselves, I am quite sure of that, but there was certainly a difference in the minds of the men who used them. Now they knew they could make hits. Now they knew they could get runs. Now they knew they could win. A new thought pattern changed the minds of those men so that the creative power of faith could operate.

Perhaps you have not been doing so well in the game of life. Perhaps you stand up to bat and cannot make a hit. You strike out time and again and your batting average is lamentably low. Let me give you a suggestion. I guarantee that it will work. The basis for my assurance is the fact that thousands of people have been trying it with very great results. Things will be very different for you if you give this method a real trial.

Start reading the New Testament and notice the number of times it refers to faith. Select a dozen of the strongest statements about faith, the ones that you like the best. Then memorise each one. Let these faith concepts drop into your conscious mind. Say them over and over again, especially just before going to sleep at night. They will sink from your conscious into your subconscious mind and in time will modify your basic thought pattern. This process will change you into a believer, and when you become such, you will in due course become an achiever. You will have new power to get what God and you decide you really want from life.

The most powerful force in human nature is the spiritual-power technique taught in the Bible. Very astutely the Bible emphasises the method by which a person can make something of himself. Faith, belief, positive thinking, faith in God, faith in other people, faith in yourself, faith in life. This is the essence of the technique that it teaches. "If thou canst believe," it says, "all things are possible to him that believeth." "If ye have faith . . . nothing shall be impossible unto you." (Matthew 17:20) "According to your faith be it unto you." (Matthew 9:29) Believe—believe—so it drives home the truth that faith moves mountains.

Some sceptical person who has never learned this powerful law of the effect of right thinking may doubt my assertions regarding the amazing results which happen when this technique is employed.

Things become better when you expect the best instead of the worst, for the reason that being freed from self-doubt, you can put your whole self into your endeavour, and nothing can stand in the way of the man who focuses his entire self on a problem. When you approach a difficulty as a personal unity, the difficulty, which itself is a demonstration of disunity, tends to deteriorate.

Expecting the best means that you put your whole heart (i.e., the central essence of your personality) into what you want to accomplish. People are defeated in life not because of lack of ability, but for lack of wholeheartedness. They do not wholeheartedly expect to succeed. Their heart isn't in it, which is to say that they themselves are not fully given. Results do not yield themselves to the person who refuses to give himself to the desired results.

A major key to success in this life, to attaining that which you deeply desire, is to be completely released and throw all there is of yourself into your studies or any project in which you are engaged. In other words, whatever you are doing, give it all you've got. Give every bit of yourself. Hold nothing back. Life cannot deny itself to the person who gives life his all. But most people, unfortunately, don't do that. In fact, very few people do, and this is a tragic cause of failure, or, if not failure, it is the reason we only half attain.

A famous Canadian athletic coach, Ace Percival, says that most people, athletes as well as non-athletes, are "holdouts," that is to say, they are always keeping something in reserve. They do not invest themselves 100 per cent in competition. Because of that fact they never achieve the highest of which they are capable.

Red Barber, famous baseball announcer, told me that he had known few athletes who completely give themselves.

Don't be a "holdout." Go all out. Do this, and life will not hold out on you.

A famous trapeze artist was instructing his students how to perform on the high trapeze bar. Finally, having given full explanations and instructions in this skill, he told them to demonstrate their ability.

One student, looking up at the insecure perch upon which he must perform, was suddenly filled with fear. He froze completely. He had a terrifying vision of himself falling to the ground. He couldn't move a muscle, so deep was his fright. "I can't do it! I can't do it!" he gasped.

The instructor put his arm around the boy's shoulder and said, "Son, you can do it, and I will tell you how." Then he made a statement which is of inestimable importance. It is one of the wisest remarks I have ever heard. He said, "Throw your heart over the bar and your body will follow."

Copy that one sentence. Write it on a card and put it in your pocket. Place it under the glass on your desk top. Tack it up on your wall. Better still, write it on your mind, you who really want to do something with life. It's packed with power, that sentence. "Throw your heart over the bar and your body will follow."

Heart is the symbol of creative activity. Fire the heart with where you want to go and what you want to be. Get it so deeply fixed in your unconscious that you will not take no for an answer, then your entire personality will follow where your heart leads. "Throw your heart over the bar" means to throw your faith over your difficulty. In other words, throw the spiritual essence of you over the bar and your material self will follow in the victory groove thus pioneered by your faith-inspired mind. Expect the best, not the worst, and you will attain your heart's desire. It is what is in the heart of you, either good or bad, strong or weak, that finally comes to you.

That this philosophy is of practical value is illustrated by an experience I had with a very young lady who came to see me one afternoon by appointment.

"I want to know why boys don't like me," she said abruptly almost before she was seated.

"Don't they?" I asked, playing for time while I looked her over.

"I'm graduating from high school this year, and I want to get married," she informed me. "But I've had only a very few dates."

"Let's analyse the situation," I suggested. "You're a pretty enough girl . . ."

"That's what I think, too," she interrupted. "Lots of girls have all the dates they want who are not as pretty as I am."

"You like to run things, don't you?" I suggested.

"I certainly do. When people don't do what they've been told to do, I believe in letting them know about it. I've been chairman of more class committees than anyone else," she added complacently.

"They make you chairman, but they don't like you," I said.

"No, they don't." For a moment her self-assurance faltered. "That's why I asked for this interview. I want you to tell me why."

I began to have hopes of her. If she was of big enough calibre to take the inevitable criticism she was asking for, maybe she would have the character to correct her personality difficulties.

"There have been boys on these committees of which you've been chairman?" She nodded. "And it has been the boys even more than the girls who have failed to carry out your commands," I guessed. Again she nodded. "Then you'd 'tell them off.' There's your answer. A boy doesn't take a girl out for a good time when he knows she'll be rough on him if things don't go to suit her, if she tries to boss him."

"You're telling me to pretend to like something I don't?" The young spine straightened; the lips of the girl's mouth pressed together in a straight firm line. "That's not honest," she informed me.

"It's kind," I suggested.

I picked up a hand mirror I have lying on my desk, for just such moments, I admit. And I held it up before her. "Look at yourself," I said. "Do you think a young man wants a wife who looks like that? Smile, Soften those lips. Make your eyes laugh. Good for you!" For she was following my suggestions. "You'd be very attractive if you'd add a little softness and generosity and kindness to your thinking.

"No man," I continued while I had her in this gentler mood that came of looking at herself in the glass, "wants a wife who tries to dominate him. He wants her to comfort him when he makes mistakes; build up his self-confidence instead of tearing it down."

Encouraged by my success, I risked going further.

"Try doing something about your hair and dress," I said.

"What's the matter with them?" she bristled.

"Too severe," I suggested. "Try to make them more alluring."

Then I told her about an old professor of mine at Ohio Wesleyan University who said, "God runs a beauty parlour." Some girls, he had told us, who were very pretty in their college days would come back to reunions not looking in the least attractive. While others, who had not been at all noticeable, would return looking quite lovely. "The beauty of an inner life was written on their faces," was his explanation. And he added, "God runs a beauty parlour."

"There's a lot in what you say," this girl admitted. "I'll try it."

And so strong was her personality that I have no doubt of her success. She had character but she needed charm. And charm comes from God.

Naturally in this process of achieving the best it is important to know where you want to go in life. You can reach your goal, your best dreams can come true, you can get where you want to go only if you know what your goal is. Your expectation must have a clearly defined objective. Lots of people get nowhere simply because they do not know where they want to go. They have no clear-cut, precisely defined purpose. You cannot expect the best if you think aimlessly.

A young man consulted me because he was dissatisfied. He was ambitious to fill a bigger niche in life and wanted to know how to improve his circumstances. His motive seemed unselfish and entirely worth while.

"Well, where do you want to go?" I asked.

"I just don't know exactly," he said hesitantly. "I have never given it any thought. I only know I want to go somewhere other than where I am."

"What can you do best?" I then asked. "What are your strong points?"

"I don't know," he responded. "I never thought that over either."

"But what would you like to do if you had your choice? What do you really want to do?" I insisted.

"I just can't say," he replied dully. "I don't really

know what I would like to do. I never thought it over. Guess I ought to figure that one out too."

"Now, look here," I said, "you want to go somewhere from where you are, but you don't know where you want to go. You don't know what you can do or what you would like to do. You will have to get your ideas organised before you can expect to start getting anywhere."

That is the failure point with many people. They never get anywhere because they have only a hazy idea where they want to go, what they want to do. No objective leads to no end.

We made a thorough analysis, testing this young man's capabilities, and found some assets of personality he did not know he possessed. But it was necessary to supply a dynamic to move him forward, so we taught him the techniques of practical faith. Today he is on the way to achievement.

Now he knows where he wants to go and how to get there. He knows what the best is and he expects to attain it and he will—nothing can stop him.

I asked an outstanding newspaper editor, an inspiring personality, "How did you get to be the editor of this important paper?"

"I wanted to be," he replied simply.

"Is that all there is to it?" I asked. "You wanted to be and so there you are."

"Well, that may not be all of it, but that was a large part of the process," he explained. "I believe that if you want to get somewhere, you must decide definitely where you want to be or what you want to accomplish. Be sure it is a right objective, then photograph this objective on your mind and hold it there. Work hard, believe in it, and the thought will become so powerful that it will tend to assure success. There is a deep tendency," he declared, "to become what your mind pictures, provided you hold the mental picture strongly enough and if the objective is sound."

So saying, the editor pulled a well-worn card from his wallet and said, "I repeat this quotation every day of my life. It has become my dominating thought."

I copied it and am giving it to you: "A man who is self-reliant, positive, optimistic, and undertakes his work with the assurance of success magnetises his condition. He draws to himself the creative powers of the universe."

So expect the best at all times. Never think of the worst. Drop it out of your thought. Let there be no thought in your mind that the worst will happen. Avoid entertaining the concept of the worst, for whatever you take into your mind can grow there. Therefore take the best into your mind and only that. Nurture it, concentrate on it, emphasise it, visualise it, prayerise it, surround it with faith. Make it your obsession. Expect the best, and spiritually creative mind power aided by God power will produce the best.

It may be that as you read this book you are down

to what you think is the worst and you may remark that no amount of thinking will affect your situation. The answer to that objection is that it simply isn't so. Even if you may be down to the worst, the best is potentially within you. You have only to find it, release it, and rise up with it. This requires courage and character, to be sure, but the main requirement is faith. Cultivate faith and you will have the necessary courage and character.

A girl was compelled by family adversity to leave school and go into sales work, a type of activity for which she had no training. She undertook to demonstrate vacuum cleaners from house to house. She took a negative attitude toward herself and her work. She "just didn't believe she could do this job." She "knew" she was going to fail. She feared to approach a house even though she came for a requested demonstration. She believed that she could not make the sale. As a result, as is not surprising, she failed in a high percentage of her interviews.

One day she chanced to call upon a woman who evidenced consideration beyond the average. To this customer the sales girl poured out her tale of defeat and powerlessness. The other woman listened patiently, then said quietly, "If you expect failure, you will get failure, but if you expect to succeed, I am sure you will succeed." And she added, "I will give you a formula which I believe will help you. It will re-style your thinking, give you new confidence, and help you to accomplish your goals. Repeat this formula before every call. Believe in it and then marvel at what it will do for you. This is it. 'If God be for us, who can be against us?' But change it by personalising it so that you say, 'If God be for *me,* who can be against *me*? If God be for me, then I know that with God's help I can sell vacuum cleaners.' God realises that you want security and support, and by practising the method I suggest, you will be given power to get what you want."

She learned to utilise this formula. She approached each house expecting to make a sale, affirming and picturising positive, not negative, results. She presently acquired new courage, new faith, and deeper confidence in her own ability. Now she declares, "God helps me sell vacuum cleaners," and who can dispute it?

Let me give you four words as a formulation of a great law—*faith power works wonders.* Those four words are packed with dynamic and creative force. Hold them in your conscious mind. Let them sink into the unconscious and they can help you to overcome any difficulty. Hold them in your thoughts, say them over and over again. Say them until your mind accepts them, until you believe them—*faith power works wonders.*

I have no doubt about the effectiveness of this concept, for I have seen it work so often that my enthusiasm for faith power is absolutely boundless.

You can overcome any obstacle. You can achieve the most tremendous things by faith power. And how do you develop faith power? The answer is: to saturate your mind with the great words of the Bible. If you will spend one hour a day reading the Bible and committing its great passages to memory, the change in you and in your experience will be little short of miraculous.

Just one section of the Bible will accomplish this for you. The eleventh chapter of Mark is enough. You will find the secret in the following words, and this is one of the greatest formulas the Book contains: "Have faith in God [that's positive, isn't it?]. For verily I say unto you, That whosoever shall say unto *this* mountain [that's specific], Be thou removed [that is, stand aside], and be thou cast into the sea [that means out of sight—anything you throw into the sea is gone for good. The steamship "Titanic" that sank years ago lies at the bottom of the sea. And the sea bottom is lined with ships. Cast your opposition called a "mountain" into the sea]; and shall not doubt in his heart [Why does this statement use the word heart? Because it means you are not to doubt in the inner essence of you. It isn't so superficial as a doubt in the conscious mind. That is a normal, intelligent questioning. It's deep fundamental doubt that is to be avoided], but shall believe that those things which he saith shall come to pass; he shall have whatsoever he saith." (Mark 11:22–23)

This is not some theory that I have thought up. It is taught by the most reliable book known to man.

Generation after generation, no matter what develops in the way of knowledge and science, the Bible is read by more people than any other book. Humanity rightly has more confidence in it than any other document ever written, and the Bible tells us that faith power works wonders.

If there is something you want, how do you go about getting it? In the first place, ask yourself, "Should I want it?" Test that question very honestly in prayer to be sure you should want it and whether you should have it. If you can answer that question in the affirmative, then ask God for it and don't be backward in asking Him. And if God, having more insight, believes that you shouldn't have it, you needn't worry—He won't give it to you. But if it is a right thing, ask Him for it; and when you ask, do not doubt in your heart. Be specific.

Be specific. Ask God for any right thing and don't doubt. Doubt closes the power flow. Faith opens it. The power of faith is so tremendous that there is nothing Almighty God cannot do for us, with us, or through us if we let Him channel His power through our minds.

Say these words over and over again until they go down deep into your heart and take possession of you: "Whosoever shall say unto this mountain, Be thou removed, and be thou cast into the sea; and shall not doubt in his heart, but shall believe that those things which he saith shall come to pass; he shall have whatsoever he saith."

I suggested these principles to the boy I spoke of at the opening of this chapter. His father had sent him to see me. In talking with him I found that he took a negative attitude towards every problem. He disbelieved everything I said but he promised to make a test of them, just to prove me wrong.

But he was an honest boy and at the end of his first year in college he came to see me again. "I didn't believe it possible," he said, "but it is a fact that if you expect the best, you are given a strange kind of power to create the conditions that produce the results you want. I've learned to expect the best and not the worst."

I might add that it is as essential to practise this attitude as it is to practise on a musical instrument, with a golf club or a tennis racket. Nobody ever mastered any skill except by intensive, persistent and intelligent practice. Every day, as you confront the day's problems, say, "I believe God gives me the power to attain what I really want." Never mention the possibility of failure; never think of it. Drop it out of your consciousness. Insist to yourself: "I expect the best and with God's help I will attain the best"—and you will. Such is the power of positive thinking.

CHAPTER 7

Be a Winner

IF YOU are a person who thinks and expects defeat, I urge you to stop and consider. For thinking defeat tends to bring it upon you. Talk to yourself; re-educate yourself; get yourself out of the habit of negative thinking, of believing anything can defeat you. I suggest that you adopt as a slogan, "Be a Winner." And say it to yourself every time doubt comes into your mind. Really believe that you can "Be a Winner."

I knew a man whom his business associates called "the obstacle man," because he met every suggestion for action with the statement: "Now just a moment. Let's consider the obstacles involved." And, with an air of wisdom, he would add, "One must always be realistic."

In one such conference the man whose plan was under discussion reached into his pocket and pulled out his wallet. "I'll show you what to do about these obstacles," he said. "We'll just remove them. And here's how." He shoved his wallet across the table about which they were sitting and pointed to a card under the plastic window. The card read: "I can do all things through Christ which strengtheneth me." (Philippians 4:13)

"I've lived a long time," said the owner of the wallet, "and faced a lot of obstacles. There's power in those words—actual power—and with them you can meet any difficulties."

He convinced his associates. His plan was put into operation and turned out successfully. Don't be an "obstacle man." If you think of an obstacle let it be only about how to break it, how to overcome it.

Winston Churchill, in his book *Maxims and Reflections*, had this to say about the British General Tudor. "The impression I had of Tudor was of an iron peg, hammered into the frozen ground, immovable." What a wonderful picture of a man. General Tudor knew how to stand up to an obstacle.

Just stand up to it: that's all. Don't let it get you, even in your thoughts. Don't give way under it, and it will finally break. You will break it. Something has to break, and it needn't be you: it can be the obstacle if you stand firm and always think positively, always visualise God as helping you.

And you can do this when you have faith, faith in God and faith in yourself. Faith is the chief quality you need. It is enough. In fact, it is more than enough.

Take the story of Gonzales, who won the national tennis championship a few years ago in a gruelling battle. He had been practically unknown, and because of wet weather he had not been able to perfect his game prior to the tournament. The sports writer of a metropolitan newspaper in analysing Gonzales said that there were certain defects in his technique, and gave it as his opinion that probably greater champions had played on the courts; however, he credited Gonzales with a marvellous serve and a skilful volley. But the factor that won the championship, said the writer, was his staying power and the further fact that "he was never defeated by the discouraging vicissitudes of the game."

That is one of the most subtle lines I have ever read in any sports story—"He was never defeated by the discouraging vicissitudes of the game."

It means, does it not, that when the game seemed to go against him he did not let discouragement creep in nor negative thoughts dominate and thus lose the power needed to win. This mental and spiritual quality made that man a champion. He was able to face obstacles, to stand up to them and overcome them.

Faith supplies staying power. It contains dynamics to keep one going when the going is hard. Anybody can keep going when the going is good, but some extra ingredient is needed to enable you to keep fighting when it seems that everything is against you. It is a great secret, that of never being "defeated by the discouraging vicissitudes of the game."

You may counter, "But you don't know my circumstances. I am in a different situation from anybody else and I am as far down as a human being can get."

In that case you are fortunate, for if you are as

far down as you can get there is no further down you can go. There is only one direction you can take from this position, and that is up. So your situation is quite encouraging. However, I caution you not to take the attitude that you are in a situation in which nobody has ever been before. There is no such situation.

Practically speaking, there are only a few human stories and they have all been enacted previously. This is a fact that you must never forget—there are people who have overcome every conceivable difficult situation, even the one in which you now find yourself and which to you seems utterly hopeless. So did it seem to some others, but they found an out, a way up, a path over, a pass through.

One of the most inspiring illustrations of this fact is the story of Amos Parrish who twice every year brings together hundreds of leading department store executives and style experts in two huge clinics held in the Grand Ballroom of the Waldorf-Astoria Hotel in New York City. At these clinics Mr. Parrish gives advice to the merchants and their associates on business trends, on merchandise, on selling methods, and other matters important to the conduct of their business. Having attended a number of the clinics, however, I am convinced that the greatest values Mr. Parrish transmits to his customers are courage and positive thinking, a deep belief in themselves, and the confidence that they can overcome all difficulties.

He seems a living example of the philosophy which he teaches. As a boy he was sickly. Moreover, he stuttered. He was sensitive and a victim of an inferiority complex. It was thought that he would not live because of his weakened physical condition, but one day Amos Parrish had a spiritual experience. Faith dawned in his mind, and from then on he knew that with the help of God and the utilisation of his own powers he could achieve.

He developed this unique idea of service to business men, and so highly do they rate it that they are willing to pay large fees to attend a two-day session twice a year under the business wisdom and inspiration of Amos Parrish. To me it is a moving experience to sit with that big crowd in a hotel ballroom and listen to "A.P.," as he is affectionately called, talk positive thinking to those important business men and women.

Sometimes he has the greatest difficulty with his stuttering, but he is never discouraged. He refers to it frankly and with a sense of humour. One day, for example, he was trying to say the word Cadillac. He tried several times and was unable to get it out, and finally did so with a powerful effort. Then he commented, "I can't even say C-C-C-Cadillac, let alone buy one." The audience roared with laughter, but I noted that they looked up at him with affection written on their faces. Everyone leaves a meeting at which he speaks with the conviction that he, too, can turn his obstacles into assets.

Again I repeat, there is no difficulty you cannot overcome. A wise and philosophical Negro once said to me, when asked how he overcame his difficulties, "How do I get through a trouble? Well, first I try to go around it, and if I can't go around it, I try and get under it, and if I can't get under it, I try to go over it, and if I can't get over it, I just plough right through it." Then he added, "God and I plough right through it."

Say seriously this formula and each time you say it conclude with the affirmation, "I believe that." Here is the formula: "I can do all things through Christ which strengtheneth me." Say that five times every day and it will release indomitable power in your mind.

Your subconscious, which always resents any change, may say to you, "You don't believe any such thing." But remember that your subconscious mind in a sense is one of the greatest liars in existence. It concurs in and sends back to you your own errors about your abilities. You have created the negative attitude in your subconscious and it gives this error back to you. So just turn on your subconscious and say to it, "Now look here, I do believe that. I insist upon believing it." If you talk to your subconscious mind with that positiveness, in due course it will be convinced. One reason is that you are now feeding it positive thoughts. In other words, you are at last telling the truth to your subconscious. After a while your subconscious mind will begin to send back the truth to you, the truth being that with the help of Jesus Christ there isn't any obstacle you cannot overcome.

An effective method for making your subconscious positive in character is to eliminate certain expressions of thought and speech which we may call the "little negatives." These so-called "little negatives" clutter up the average person's conversation, and while each one is seemingly unimportant in itself, the total effect of these attitudes is to condition the mind negatively. When this thought of "little negatives" first occurred to me, I began to analyse my own conversational habits and was shocked by what I found. I discovered I was making such statements as, "I'm afraid I'll be late," or "I wonder if I'll have a flat tyre," or "I don't think I can do that," or "I'll never get through this job. There's so much to do." If something turned out badly, I might say, "Oh, that's just what I expected." Or again, I might observe a few clouds in the sky and would gloomily state, "I know it is going to rain."

These are "little negatives" to be sure, and a big thought is of course more powerful than a little one, but it must never be forgotten that "mighty oaks from little acorns grow," and if a mass of "little negatives" clutter up your conversation, they are bound to seep into your mind. It is surprising how they accumulate in force, and presently, before you know it, they will grow into "big negatives." So I determined to go to work on the "little negatives" and root them out from my conversation. I found that the best way to eliminate them was deliberately to say a positive word about everything. When you keep asserting that things are going to work out well, that you can do the job, that you will not have a flat tyre, that you will get there on time, by talking up good results you invoke the law of positive effects and good results occur. Things do turn out well.

On a roadside billboard I saw an advertisement of a certain brand of motor oil. The slogan read, "A clean engine always delivers power." So will a mind free of negatives produce positives: that is to say, a clean mind will deliver power. Therefore flush out your thoughts, give yourself a clean mental engine, remembering that a clean mind, even as a clean engine, always delivers power.

So to overcome your obstacles and live the "Be a Winner" philosophy, cultivate a positive-idea pattern deeply in your consciousness. What we do with obstacles is directly determined by our mental attitude. Most of our obstacles, as a matter of fact, are mental in character.

"Ah," you may object, "mine are not mental, mine are real."

Perhaps so, but your attitude toward them is mental. The only possible way you can have an attitude is by the mental process, and what you think about your obstacles largely determines what you do about them. Form the mental attitude that you cannot remove an obstacle and you will not remove it, not if you think you can't. But get the idea firmly fixed that the obstacle is not so great as you previously considered it to be. Hold the idea that it is removable; and however faintly you entertain this positive thought, from the very moment you begin to think in this manner, the process is started which will lead to its removal.

If you have been long defeated by a difficulty, it is probably because you have told yourself for weeks, months, and even for years that there is nothing you can do about it. And when your mind is convinced, you are convinced, for as you think so are you.

But on the contrary, when you employ this new and creative concept, "I can do all things through Christ," then you develop a new mental slant. Emphasise and re-emphasise that positive attitude and you will finally convince your own consciousness that you can do something about difficulties. When at last your mind becomes convinced, astonishing results will begin to happen. Of a sudden you discover that you have the power you would never acknowledge.

I played golf recently with a young man who was not only an excellent golfer, but a bit of a philosopher as well. As we went around the golf course, the game itself drew out of him certain gems of wisdom, for one of which I shall ever be grateful.

I hit a ball into the rough, into some high grass. When we came up to my ball I said in some dismay, "Now just look at that. I certainly am in the rough.

I have a bad lie. It is going to be tough getting out of here."

My friend grinned and said, "Didn't I read something about positive thinking in your books?"

Sheepishly I acknowledged that such was the case.

"I wouldn't think negatively about that lie of yours," he said. "Do you think you could get a good hit if this ball were lying out on the fairway on the short grass?"

I said I thought so.

"Well," he continued, "why do you think you could do better out there than here?"

"Because," I replied, "the grass is cut short on the fairway and the ball can get away better."

Then he did a curious thing. "Let's get down on our hands and knees," he suggested, "and examine the situation. Let's see just how this ball does lie."

So we got down on our hands and knees, and he said, "Observe that the relative height of the ball here is about the same as it would be on the fairway, the only difference being that you have about five or six inches of grass above the ball."

Then he did an even more whimsical thing. "Notice the quality and character of this grass," he said. He pulled off a blade and handed it to me. "Chew it," he said.

I chewed, and he asked, "Isn't that tender?"

"Why, yes," I replied. "It certainly does seem to be tender grass."

"Well," he continued, "an easy swing of your

number five iron will cut through that grass almost like a knife." And then he gave me this sentence which I am going to remember as long as I live, and I hope you will also:

"The rough is only mental.

"In other words," he continued, "it is rough because you think it is. In your mind you have decided that here is an obstacle which will cause you difficulty. The power to overcome this obstacle is in your mind. If you visualise yourself lifting that ball out of the rough, believing you can do it, your mind will transfer flexibility, rhythm, and power to your muscles and you will handle that club in such a manner that the ball will rise out of there in a beautiful shot. All you need to do is to keep your eye on that ball and tell yourself that you are going to lift it out of that grass with a lovely stroke. Let the stiffness and tension go out of you. Hit it with exhilaration and power. Remember, the rough is only mental."

To this day I remember the thrill, the sense of power and delight I had in the clean shot that dropped the ball to the edge of the green.

That is a very great fact to remember in connection with difficult problems—"the rough is only mental."

Your obstacles are present all right. They are not fanciful, but they are not actually so difficult as they seem. Your mental attitude is the most important factor. Believe that Almighty God has put in you the power to lift yourself out of the rough by keeping your eye firmly fixed on the source of your power. Affirm to yourself that through this power you can do anything you have to do. Believe this, and a sense of victory will come.

Now take another look at that obstacle that has been bothering you. You will find that it isn't so formidable as you thought. Say to yourself, "The rough is only mental. I think victory—I get victory." Remember that formula. Write it on a card, put it in your wallet, or behind your mirror in your handbag, put it on your dressing-table or on your desk—keep looking at it until its truth permeates your whole mental attitude—"I can do all things through Christ which strengtheneth me."

Let me give you a striking illustration of how this positive principle worked in one case. It can be the same in any situation.

In a little Texas town an eight-year-old boy was playing ball. Suddenly he dropped to the ground unable to move. From then on for years it was a battle against infantile paralysis. But Walter Davis won that battle as is sufficiently indicated by the fact that he became the World's Champion High Jumper.

From the day he started jumping his ambition was to win that championship. Accordingly he gave it all he had.

Constant practice, training for physical perfection, built him into a strong boy, tall and athletic.

He had married the girl next door and she was

good and also wise and she said, "There's another kind of strength even the strongest man needs, the strength of belief. Without it a man is nothing." With her help Walter Davis acquired that strength.

Came the day of the big championship event. His opponent cleared the bar at 6 feet 10¾ inches. Davis got over at 6 feet 11 inches. They raised the bar to 11½ inches. He made it, then it was raised to the new high not previously attained of 6 feet 11⅝ inches. Twice he tried but shook the bar loose. Only three tries are allowed. Davis sat on the ground and looked up at the bar. The packed stadium was hushed.

He bowed his head and asked for spiritual strength, that extra something beyond physical power, that extra quality that makes real champions. With God's power working in him he cleared the bar to become champion high jumper of the world.

"And," says Champion Davis, "the biggest jump I ever made was when I discovered it's easy and natural to pray."

Thomas Jefferson had a saying which I think priceless: "Always take hold of things by the smooth handle." That is, examine your problem and go at it in such a way as to encounter the least resistance. Resistance causes friction and the negative attitude is a friction approach. Negativism develops resistance. The positive approach is the "smooth handle" technique. It is in harmony with the flow of the universe. It not only encounters less resistance; it actually stimulates assistant forces.

For example, a mother sent her fifteen-year-old son to us. She said she wanted him "straightened out." It annoyed her no end that her boy could never get over 70 in any of his studies. "This boy has a great mind potentially," she declared proudly.

"How do you know he has a great mind?" I asked.

"Because he is my son," she said. "I graduated from college *magna cum laude*."

The boy came in very glumly, so I asked, "What's the matter, son?"

"I don't know. My mother sent me to see you."

"Well," I commented, "you don't seem to be burning with enthusiasm. Your mother says you only get 70's."

"Yes," he said, "That's all I get, and," he added, "that isn't the worst of it. I've even received less than that."

"Do you think you have a good mind, son?" I asked.

"My mother says I have. I don't know—I think I'm awful dumb. Dr. Peale," he said earnestly, "I study the stuff. At home I read it over once and then close the book and try to remember it. I repeat this process about three times, and then I think that if three times doesn't get it into my head, how am I ever going to get it into my head? And then I go to school thinking maybe I have it, and the teacher calls on me to say something, and I stand up and can't remember a thing. Then," he said, "examinations come along and I sit there and just get hot and cold all over and I can't think of the answers. I don't know why," he continued. "I know that my mother was a great scholar. I guess I just haven't got it in me."

This negative thought pattern combined with the inferiority feeling stimulated by his mother's attitude was of course defeating him. He froze up in his mind. His mother had never told him to go to school and study for the wonder and glory of learning knowledge. She was not wise enough to encourage him to compete with himself rather than with others. And she was constantly insisting that he duplicate her success in scholarship. Little wonder that under this pressure he froze mentally.

I gave him some suggestions that proved helpful. "Before you read your lessons, pause a moment and pray in this manner, 'Lord, I know I have a good mind and that I can get my work.' Then get yourself relaxed and read the book without strain. Imagine you are reading a story. Do not read it twice unless you wish. Simply believe that you got it on the first reading. Visualise the material as soaking in and germinating. Then next morning, as you go to school, say to yourself, 'I have a wonderful mother. She is very pretty and sweet, but she must have been an old bookworm to get those high marks. And who wants to be an old bookworm anyway? I don't want to become *magna cum* anything. I only want to get through school creditably.'

"In class, when the teacher calls on you, quickly

pray before answering. Then believe the Lord will at that moment help your mind to deliver. When an examination is given, affirm in prayer that God is releasing your mind and that the right answers are given you."

The boy followed these ideas, and what marks do you think he got the following semester? Ninety! I am sure that this boy, having discovered the amazing workability of the "I don't believe in defeat" philosophy, will employ the amazing power of positive thinking in all the affairs of his life.

I could use so many illustrations of the manner in which young people's lives have been helped by these procedures that this book would grow to unwieldy size. Moreover, these are incidents and experiences out of everyday life that are in no way theoretical, but are entirely practical. My mail is literally filled with testimonials sent by people who have felt moved to relate similar occurrences in their own lives.

Such a letter came from a gentleman who tells about his father. I know several people who have used the plan in this matter with amazing results:

> My father was a travelling salesman. One time he sold furniture, another time hardware, sometimes it was leather goods. He changed his line every year.
>
> I would hear him telling Mother that this was his last trip in stationery or in bed lamps or whatever it was he was selling at the moment. Next

year everything would be different; we would be on Easy Street. He had a chance to go with a firm that had a product that sold itself. It was always the same. My father never had a product that sold. He was always tense, always afraid of himself, always whistling in the dark.

Then one day a fellow salesman gave Father a copy of a little three-sentence prayer. He was told to repeat it just before calling on a customer. Father tried it, and the results were almost miraculous. He sold 85 per cent of all calls made during the first week, and every week thereafter the results were wonderful. Some weeks the percentage ran as high as 95, and Father had sixteen weeks in which he sold every customer called on.

Father gave this prayer to several other salesmen, and in each case it brought astounding results.

The prayer my father used is as follows:

"I believe I am always divinely guided.

"I believe I will always take the right turn of the road.

"I believe God will always make a way where there is no way."

The head of a small firm who had a great many difficulties in establishing his business told me that he was immeasurably helped by a technique which he invented. He had trouble, he said, with the tendency to "blow up" a small difficulty into a seemingly insurmountable obstacle. He knew that he was approaching his problems in a defeatist attitude, and had common sense enough to realise that these obstacles were not so difficult as he made them appear to be. So he simply placed a large wire basket on his office desk. The following words were printed on a card and wired to this basket, "With God all things are possible." Whenever a problem came up which began to develop into a big difficulty, he threw the paper pertaining to it into the basket marked "With God all things are possible" and let it rest there for a day or two. "It is queer how each matter when I took it out of that basket again didn't seem difficult at all," he reported.

In this act he dramatised the mental attitude of putting the problem in God's hands. As a result he received power to handle the problem normally and therefore successfully.

As you finish this chapter please say the following line aloud: "With God's help I'm a winner."

Continue to affirm that until the idea dominates your subconscious attitudes.

CHAPTER 8

Why Worry?

WHAT is worry? It is simply an unhealthy and destructive mental habit. If you have it, you were not born with it: you acquired it. And since you can change any habit, you can cast worry from your mind. So let's start breaking your worry habit at once.

Haven't you often heard a person say, "I am almost sick with worry"; and then add with a laugh, "But I guess worry never really makes you ill." But that is where he is wrong. Worry can make you ill. A doctor recently stated that there is an epidemic of fear and worry in this country. "All doctors," he declared, "are having cases of illness brought on directly by fear, and aggravated by worry."

What worry can do to you is indicated by the original meaning of the word itself. It comes from an old Anglo-Saxon word meaning to "choke." If someone were to put his fingers around your throat and press hard, cutting off your air supply, he would be doing to you dramatically what you do to yourself over a long period of time by worry. You choke your abilities, your health, your creative powers.

Imagination is a source of fear, but imagination

may also be a cure of fear. Your little brother or sister possesses an imaginative skill superior to your own. You've seen him stop crying because your mother has kissed the spot that hurt. Imagination is not simply the use of fancy. The word imagination derives from the idea of using images or pictures; you form an image or mental picture either of fear or of release from fear. If your little niece is afraid of a dog, she can be talked out of her fear by being told the dog is only trying to be friends, likes her, wants to kiss her. What you "image" (imagine) may become a fact if held mentally with sufficient faith.

Therefore, hold an image of yourself as being free from worry. Suppose your English teacher has assigned a paper for you to write: something like "Trees I Know." And you don't know anything about trees. What do you do? You start worrying. You talk about it to everybody you know. Days pass, and you've done nothing about writing that paper except to worry about it. You don't have to be like that. Instead of worrying, imagine yourself as a person who is interested in trees, who wants to find out about trees, who looks at them and talks about them and reads about them. Before you know it, you will be the person whom you have imagined. You'll be able to write that paper and enjoy it.

Or are you a person who is afraid of thunderstorms? That is something that can make you wretched, something you'd better get rid of: for you can. Fear is the most powerful of all thoughts with one exception, and that one exception is faith. Faith can always overcome fear. So when you find in yourself the impulse to hide in a dark cupboard when you hear the thunder beginning to rumble, start talking to yourself. Say aloud, if it is possible, "God is now filling my mind with courage, with peace, with calm. God is now protecting me from all harm. I have no fear for God will see me through this storm." How amazingly beautiful nature is when a great storm sweeps across the world and colossal power is demonstrated.

Form the habit of asserting your possession of faith. Hold an image of yourself as delivered from worry, and a mental drainage process will in time eliminate abnormal fear from your thoughts. However, it is not enough to empty the mind, for the mind will not long stay empty. It must be occupied by something. It cannot continue in a state of vacuum. Therefore, upon emptying the mind, practise refilling it. Fill it with thoughts of faith, hope, courage, expectancy. Say aloud such affirmations as the following: "God is now filling my mind with courage, with peace, with calm assurance. God is now protecting me from all harm. God is now protecting my loved ones from all harm. God is now guiding me to right decisions. God will see me through this situation."

A half-dozen times each day crowd your mind with such thoughts as these until the mind is overflowing with them. In due course these thoughts of faith will crowd out worry. Day by day, as you fill your mind with faith, there will ultimately be no room left for fear. This is the one great fact that no one should forget. Master faith and you will automatically master fear.

So the process is—empty the mind and cauterise it of fear with God's grace, then practise filling your mind with faith and you will break the worry habit. It will not be of much value merely to read this suggestion unless you practise it. And the time to begin practising it is now while you think of it and while you are convinced that the number one procedure in breaking the worry habit is to drain the mind daily of fear, and fill the mind daily with faith. It is just as simple as that. Learn to be a practiser of faith until you become an expert in faith. Then fear cannot live in you.

The importance of freeing your mind of fear cannot be over-emphasised. Fear something over a long period of time and there is a real possibility that you may help bring it to pass. The Bible contains a line, terrible in its truth: "For the thing which I greatly feared is come upon me . . ." (Job 3:25) Of course it will. If you fear something continuously you tend to create the conditions in your mind propitious to the development of that which you fear. An atmosphere is encouraged in which it can take root and grow.

But the Bible also reiterates another great truth, in substance: "That which I have greatly believed has come upon me." It does not make that statement in so many words; yet again and again it tells us that if we have faith "nothing is impossible" to us, and "according to your faith be it done unto you." So if you shift your mind from fear to faith you will stop creating the object of your fear and will instead make actual for yourself the object of your faith. Surround your mind with thoughts of faith and not fear and you will produce faith results instead of fear results.

Strategy must be used in the campaign against the worry habit. A subtle and successful attack on fear is to snip off the little worries, one by one, before going at the main trunk of your fear.

At my farm it was necessary to take down a large tree, much to my regret. Cutting down a great old tree is fraught with sadness. Men came with a motor-driven saw and I expected them to start by cutting through the main trunk near the ground. Instead, they put up ladders and began snipping off the small branches, then the larger ones, and finally the top of the tree. Then all that remained was the huge central trunk, and in a few moments my tree lay neatly stacked as though it had not spent fifty years in growing.

"If we had cut the tree at the ground before trimming off the branches, it would have broken nearby trees in falling. It is easier to handle a tree the smaller you can make it." So explained the tree man.

Thus, if you have acquired the habit of worry, you can handle it best in this way. Snip off the little worries. Watch the worry-words in your conversation: they are the result of worry, but they also create worry. Don't say, "I'm afraid it will rain today; see that cloud on the horizon?" Say, instead, "Nice to have a bit of blue sky, isn't it?" Let the rest of the day take care of itself. Instead of worrying about being late for school, or for the school bus, start early. That will leave your mind uncluttered and it can occupy itself with more important items like posture—walk with a free and easy pace; or the expression on your face—is it pleasant and smiling?

Snipping off small worries will help you to develop power to deal with the habit of worry. In time the impulse towards worry will wither and die.

Another strategy is to play a game with worry. Worry cannot win against you when you see that it isn't as strong as it seems.

Worry always seems worse than it actually is. That is why it is so fearsome. Most of it is bluff; nothing to it. I once knew an old man who told me he had kept a worry score card and that 92 per cent of the things he had worried about over his lifetime never happened. The other 8 per cent, he said, he had been able to meet and deal with quite well through God's help.

Another man was very clever in dealing with all the things we worry about but which never happen. He organised what he called the "Wednesday Worry

Club." He was the only member and all the officers. The "club" met every Wednesday night at 8 o'clock. All week long every time a worry came he wrote it on a piece of paper and put it in a big "worry box" to be worried about at the club meeting. When each Wednesday night at 8 o'clock he opened the box and looked at all the worries he discovered that 90 per cent of them hadn't happened. So he threw them in the waste paper basket.

But what about the 10 per cent that were still live? He put them back in the worry box to be worried about next Wednesday at 8 p.m. So you will do well to take a sort of amused and sensible attitude toward that great big almost empty ghost called worry that frightens so many people needlessly out of their wits.

My friend Dr. Daniel A. Poling, editor of the *Christian Herald*, gives a valuable suggestion. He says that every morning he repeats these two words, "I believe," three times. Thus at the day's beginning he conditions his mind to faith, and it never leaves him. His mind accepts the conviction that by faith he is going to overcome his problems and difficulties during the day. He starts the day with creative positive thoughts in his mind. He "believes," and it is very difficult to hold back the man who believes.

I related Dr. Poling's technique in a radio talk and I had a letter from a woman who said she had not been very faithful in practising her religion and she decided to try Dr. Poling's "I believe." She said her husband was out of work; her mother-in-law who lived with them complained constantly of her aches and pains; there was continual bickering in the house. "It has only been ten days," her letter said, "since I started this plan. My husband came home last night saying he had a job paying eighty dollars a week. And my mother-in-law has practically stopped complaining. It is like a miracle. My worries have disappeared."

This does seem magical, yet it happens every day to people who shift over from negative fear thoughts to positive faith thoughts.

The late Howard Chandler Christy, the famous artist, had a sound anti-worry technique. "Don't you ever worry?" I asked him.

"I don't believe in it," he said.

"Haven't you ever worried?" I persisted.

"Yes," he said. "I tried it once. I noticed that everybody else seemed to worry and I figured I must be missing something. So I set aside a day and I said, 'This is my worry day.'

"The night before, I went to bed early to be rested up to do a good job of worrying. I got up and ate a good breakfast—you can't worry successfully on an empty stomach—and then decided to get to my worrying. I tried my best to worry until along about noon. But I just couldn't make head nor tail of it. It didn't make sense to me, so I just gave it up."

He laughed his infectious laugh.

"You must have some other method of overcoming worry," I persisted. He did indeed, and it is perhaps the best method of all.

"Every morning I spend fifteen minutes filling my mind full of God," he said. "When my mind is full of God, there is no room for worry."

A young man who had recently inherited his father's business nearly worried himself into ill health. He was what I call a post-mortem worrier; he was always doubtful as to whether he had done or said the right thing.

Then he decided to break himself of the worry habit. "I've finally got the secret of it," he said to me. "Come to my office some day about quitting time and I'll show you something."

I did just that. By the door of his office stood a waste paper basket and above it on the wall one of those calendars where you see just one day at a time; and that date was in large print, I noticed. He said, "Now I will perform my evening ritual, the one that has helped me break the worry habit."

He reached up and tore off the calendar page for that particularly day. He rolled it into a small ball and I watched with fascination as his fingers slowly opened and he dropped that "day" into the waste paper basket. Then he closed his eyes and his lips moved, and I knew that he was praying, so was respectfully silent. Upon finishing his prayer he said aloud, "Amen. O.K., the day is over. Come on, let's go out and enjoy ourselves."

As we walked down the street I asked, "Would

you mind telling me what you said in that prayer?"

He laughed and said, "I don't think it is your kind of prayer." But I persisted, and he said, "Well, I pray something like this: 'Lord, you gave me this day. I didn't ask for it, but I was glad to have it. I did the best I could with it and you helped me, and I thank you. I made some mistakes. That was when I didn't follow your advice, and I am sorry about that. Forgive me. But I had some victories and some successes, too, and I am grateful for your guidance. But now, Lord, mistakes or successes, victories or defeats, the day is over and I'm through with it, so I'm giving it back to you. Amen.' "

To conclude this chapter in a manner designed to help you stop worrying, I list eight points, techniques that have proved helpful to other young people.

1. Say to yourself: "Worry is just a very bad habit. I can change any habit with God's help."

2. You became a worrier by practising worry. You can become free of worry by practising the opposite and stronger habit of faith. With all the strength and perseverance you can command, start practising faith.

3. How do you practise faith? Every morning say out loud, "I believe." Say it three times.

4. Pray, using this formula: "I place this day in the Lord's hands. Whatever happens, if I am in the Lord's hands it is the Lord's will and it is good."

5. Practise saying something positive concerning everything. Do not talk negatively. Don't say, "This day's going to be tough." Say, "I'm going to enjoy this day." Don't say, "I'll never be able to do what I have to do today." Say, "With God's help I can do it."

6. Never take part in a worry conversation. A group of people talking pessimistically can infect every person in the group. By talking things up rather than down you can drive away that depressing atmosphere and make everybody else feel hopeful and happy.

7. Cultivate friendships with hopeful people.

8. Every day conceive of yourself as living in partnership and companionship with Jesus Christ. Imagine Him walking by your side and saying, "I am with you always." Believe that you will never worry or be afraid.

CHAPTER 9

Ten Ways to Solve Your Problems

EVERY problem can be solved. Believe that, and the suggestions you will find in this chapter will help. Let me tell you a story.

I had known Bill Adams—I'll call him that—all through his pre-college years and I had realised that his hours in the classroom were endured only as the price he was asked to pay to make him eligible for football and baseball. Bill was good at his studies, too. Only nothing interested him that went on indoors.

When he entered college it was a foregone conclusion among all of us who had attended the games in which he starred that Bill would make both first teams. But Bill, for the first time in his young life, was up against really stiff competition. There were other boys who had been stars, too, in their home-town schools. When he became a sophomore, there was only one position on either of the first teams open that year and Bill was only as good as, not better than, several others.

Anyway, another boy won the football position and Bill came home for his Christmas holiday as unhappy and discouraged a boy as I ever saw. There was resentment among all his friends, old as well as young; and the general conviction was expressed that Bill had been the victim of favouritism, undue outside influence, and personal prejudice. There was a growing sentiment among Bill's intimates that he should change at mid-year to another college, a school where one of Bill's former team-mates—a boy who had never equalled Bill's prowess—had made the first team.

Bill came to see me to talk things over. With him came a girl, Mary, who was not only Bill's violent partisan but who had a personal motive since she, herself, was expecting to enter the second and smaller school the following autumn.

I suggested that what we needed was divine guidance, a wisdom beyond ourselves in this situation. There was such an emotional content in the problem that we might possibly be incapable of thinking the matter through objectively and rationally.

I suggested therefore that we have a few minutes of quietness, no one saying anything; that we sit in an attitude of fellowship and prayer, turning our thoughts to One who said, "Where two or three are gathered together in my name, there am I in the midst of them." (Matthew 18:20) I pointed out that there were three of us, and if we sought to achieve the spirit of being gathered in His name, He would also be present to show us what to do.

Presently, after a few minutes, I suggested that we join hands. Then I prayed quietly and asked for guidance. I prayed for peace of mind for Bill and for Mary. I went a step further and asked God's blessing on the boy who had received the spot on the team for which Bill had longed. And I prayed that Bill would take his place in his school's activities and give effective service.

After the prayer we sat silent for a time.

Then, a little ruefully, Mary spoke. "I think I knew it would turn out like this when Bill asked me to come along. I knew you'd tell us to take the Christian attitude."

"I never meant to run away," Bill, whom I had always trusted, said. "But I did want Mary to feel better about it. I'll go back and I'll help all I can."

As it turned out, Bill did help in a most effective and unexpected way. This other boy—I'll call him Andrew—and Bill were pledged to the same fraternity. Bill was so much the better student that the other boy might have failed to pass his examinations, thereby losing both his position on the team and his fraternity initiation, if Bill hadn't coached him.

When Bill came home for the Easter holiday it was another story. "We're both going to make the baseball team," he said. "Andy and I sort of key each other up; coach likes us. As for next year," he smiled his gentle smile, "guess we'll manage to stay together in football, too. Coach has just promised that."

Then Bill made a statement that I treasure. "Christianity really works, doesn't it?" he said.

One of the basic truths taught by the Bible is that God is with us. Christianity teaches that in all the difficulties, problems and circumstances of this life, God is close by. We can talk to Him, lean on Him, get help from Him.

In getting correct solutions to your problems it is necessary to go a step further than believing this: one must actually practise the idea of God's presence. Believe that God is as real as your closest friend: that He hears what you say to Him, and gives thought to the problem you put up to Him. If you believe and practise that faith, your solution will be correct, you will be guided to the truth, and things will come out right.

A business man, a friend of mine, told me of a period when it looked as if he were going to lose his store. He was a retail merchant. His stock wasn't moving, he owed money, his clerks were lazy and uninterested. "I guess they smelled failure," was the way he put it.

"I went into my office one day," he said, "so depressed that I actually thought of blowing my brains out. I shut the door, sat down in my chair, and put my head on my arms on the desk. And I certainly did pray. Then I thought of a suggestion I had often heard you make, that one can take God as a partner. So I told the Lord I was sunk, that I couldn't get any ideas but panicky ones, that I was bewildered and discouraged. 'I don't even know how You are going to tell me what to do,' I said. 'But I'm ready to hear and I'll follow Your advice as my partner if You will make it clear.'

"That was the prayer," he said. "After I'd finished I sat there waiting for the miracle; but nothing happened. However, I did feel suddenly quiet and rested. I actually had a feeling of peacefulness. I began to feel that things would turn out right. Nothing was any different. But I was different.

"I kept praying each day, not churchy prayers, just plain man-to-man talk with God. And suddenly one day an idea for moving my stock popped up in my mind, the way toast pops up in a toaster. 'What do you know about that?' I said to myself. Why I hadn't thought of that idea before I can't guess. Perhaps my mind was too panicky to think, all tied up. I hadn't been functioning mentally. Anyway the idea was good; it worked. And my business was out of the red."

That incident is just one of many. I cannot emphasise too strongly the effectiveness of this technique of problem solving. It is necessary first of all to believe that you have within you the answer. And then you must get into contact with God so that He can guide you to that answer.

Another business man friend of mine puts it this way. He says he puts his dependence on "the emergency powers of the human brain." It is his theory, and a sound one, that a human being has extra abilities that may be tapped in an emergency.

You know how races are won. The winner isn't

always the boy who gets out in front at the starting gun and runs ahead of the field. He is more likely to be that contestant who has a final reserve of power —which is mental rather than physical—which he can call on at the last moment. Haven't you, when you were tired almost to the point of exhaustion, found that you could always drive yourself just a little bit further, a little bit longer? In ordinary day-by-day living these emergency powers lie dormant. But under extraordinary circumstances we are all able to deliver that extra spurt if needed. It is that extra *spiritual* force that makes champions.

I heard a lecturer once defend the activities of a mountaineers' club by saying that such climbing developed the body—lungs and heart—and made it better able to withstand later calls upon it. "Anger is not so likely to tax your ability at self-control if your body is trained to sudden strain and stress," he said.

I don't vouch for the truth of that; I wouldn't say that I had found athletes any safer from attacks of bad temper than others. But I do claim that the person who develops a working faith has a pipeline to these dormant powers when he needs them. They have made it a daily habit to draw upon God.

When trouble comes, do you know how to meet it? Have you a plan already developed? Or do you try the hit-or-miss method that misses more often than it hits? In addition to the two techniques already suggested, that of two or three praying together, and the one of tapping emergency powers, here is a third: I call it practising faith. I read the Bible for years before it ever dawned on me that it was trying to tell me that if I would have faith—and really have it—I could overcome all of my difficulties, meet every situation, rise above every defeat, and solve all of the perplexing problems of my life. The day that dawned on me was one of the greatest, if not the greatest, of my life. Undoubtedly many people will read this book who have never got the faith idea of living. But I hope you will get it now, for it is without question one of the most powerful truths in the world for the successful conduct of human life.

Throughout the Bible the truth is emphasised again and again that "If ye have faith as a grain of mustard seed . . . nothing shall be impossible unto you." (Matthew 17:20) The Bible means this absolutely. It isn't a fantasy. It is not an illustration, nor a metaphor, but the absolute fact—faith, even as a grain of mustard seed, will solve your problems, any of your problems, all of your problems, if you believe it and practise it. "According to your faith be it unto you." (Matthew 9:29) The requirement is faith, and directly in proportion to the faith that you have and use will you get results. Little faith gives you little results, medium faith gives you medium results, great faith gives you great results. But in the generosity of Almighty God, if you have only the faith symbolised by a grain of mustard seed, it will do amazing things in solving your problems.

For example, let me tell you the thrilling story of my friends Maurice and Mary Alice Flint. I became acquainted with them when a prevous book of mine, *A Guide to Confident Living,** was condensed in *Liberty* magazine. Maurice Flint not only was failing in his job, but as a person as well. He was one of the most negative individuals I have ever encountered; he was endowed with a nice personality and at heart was a wonderful fellow.

He read the condensation of the book in which is emphasised the idea of "mustard-seed faith." At this time he was living in Philadelphia with his family, a wife and two sons. He telephoned my church in New York, but for some reason did not make contact with my secretary. I mention this for normally he would never have called the second time, because it was his pathetic habit to give up everything after a feeble effort. The next Sunday he drove from Philadelphia to New York with his family to attend church.

In an interview later, he told me his life story. The problems of money, of situations, of debts, of the future, and primarily of himself were so complicated and he was so overwhelmed with difficulty that he regarded the situation as completely hopeless.

I assured him that if he would get himself straightened out and get his mental attitudes attuned to

* World's Work Ltd.

God's pattern of thought, and learn the technique of faith, all of his problems could be solved.

One attitude he had to clear out of his mind was resentment. He was dully mad at everybody and not because of any failure on his part but because of "dirty deals" other people had given him. He and his wife actually used to lie in bed at night telling each other what they would like to say to other people by way of insult. In this unhealthy atmosphere they tried to find sleep and rest.

The faith idea gripped Flint as nothing ever had. At first he was unable to think with any power due to his long habit of negativism, but he held on tenaciously to the idea that if you have faith as a grain of mustard seed, nothing is impossible. With what force he did have he absorbed faith.

One evening he went into the kitchen where his wife was washing dishes. He said, "The faith idea is comparatively easy on Sunday in church, but I can't hold it. It fades. I was thinking that if I could carry a mustard seed in my pocket, I could feel it when I begin to weaken and that would help me to have faith." He then asked his wife, "Do we have any of those mustard seeds, or are they just something mentioned in the Bible? Are there mustard seeds today?"

She laughed and said, "I have some right here in a pickle jar."

She fished one out and gave it to him. "Don't you know, Maurice," Mary Alice said, "that you don't need an actual mustard seed. That is only the symbol of an idea."

"I don't know about that," he replied. "It says mustard seed in the Bible and that's what I want. Maybe I need the symbol to get faith."

He looked at it in the palm of his hand and said wonderingly, "Is that all the faith I need—just a small amount like this tiny grain of mustard seed?" He held it for a while and then put it in his pocket, saying, "If I can just get my fingers on that during the day, it will keep me working on this faith idea." But the seed was so small he lost it, and he would go back to the pickle jar for another one, only to lose it also. One day when another seed became lost, the idea came to him, why couldn't he put the grain of mustard seed into a plastic ball?

He consulted a supposed expert in plastics and asked. The "expert" said it could not be done for the reason that it had never been done.

Flint had enough faith by this time to believe that if he had faith "even as a grain of mustard seed" he could put a mustard seed in a plastic sphere. He went to work, and kept at it for weeks, and finally succeeded. He made up several pieces of costume jewellery—necklace, bow pin, key chain, bracelet—and sent them to me. They were beautiful, and on each gleamed the translucent sphere with the mustard seed within. With each one was a card which bore the title, "Mustard Seed Remembrancer." The card also told how this piece of jewellery could be used; how the mustard seed would remind the wearer that if he had faith, nothing was impossible.

He asked me if I thought these articles could be merchandised. I was a bit doubtful, and showed them to Grace Oursler, consulting editor of *Guideposts* magazine. She took the jewellery to Walter Hoving, president of Bonwit Teller Department Store. Imagine my delight when in the New York papers a few days later appeared an advertisement reading, "Symbol of faith—a genuine mustard seed enclosed in sparkling glass makes a bracelet with real meaning." And in the advertisement was the Scripture passage, "If ye have faith as a grain of mustard seed . . . nothing shall be impossible unto you." Now hundreds of department stores and shops throughout the country find difficulty keeping them in stock.

Mr. and Mrs. Flint have a factory in a Midwestern city producing Mustard Seed Remembrancers. Curious, isn't it—a failure goes to church and hears a text out of the Bible, and creates a great business. Perhaps you had better listen more intently to the reading of the Bible and the sermon the next time you go to church. Perhaps you, too, will get an idea that will not only rebuild your life but will give you creative practical ideas as well.

The effect on Maurice and Mary Alice Flint—the transformation of their lives, the re-making of their characters, the releasing of their personalities—this is a thrilling demonstration of faith power. They have overcome resentment and their hearts are filled with love. They are new people with a new outlook and a new sense of power.

Ask Maurice and Mary Alice Flint how to get a problem solved right. They will tell you: "Have faith—really have faith." And believe me, they know.

If as you read this story you have said to yourself negatively, "The Flints were never so badly off as I am," let me tell you that I have scarcely ever seen anybody as badly off as were the Flints. And let me say further that, however desperate your situation may be, if you will use the techniques outlined in this chapter, you, too, can get your problem solved.

Now I wish to give ten simple suggestions to use whenever you have a problem to solve.

1. Believe that for every problem there is a solution.

2. Keep calm. Your brain cannot operate efficiently under stress. Go at your problem easy like.

3. Don't try to force an answer. Keep your mind relaxed so that the solution will become clear when the right time comes.

4. Get all the facts together; look at them without bias. Try to judge them as if they were no personal concern of yours.

5. Write down these facts on a sheet of paper. When you do this and get them into proper order,

you will see them and then think about them more clearly.

6. Pray about your problems. Say and believe that God will bring light into your mind.

7. Seek God's guidance on the promise in the 73rd Psalm, "Thou shalt guide me with thy counsel."

8. Trust in the faculty of insight and intuition.

9. Go to church and let your subconscious mind work on the problem. Spiritual thinking has amazing power to give "right" answers.

10. If you follow these steps faithfully, then the answer that develops in your mind, or comes to pass, is the right answer to your problem. Believe that.

CHAPTER 10

What to Do in a Slump

Do you ever feel let down, and without any particular reason? Of course there is a reason: something that has happened, or something that somebody has said, or perhaps just the reacting from over-excitement. But it isn't a pleasant state to be in. And there are things that can be done about it.

The manner in which spiritual and emotional vitality can be restored is illustrated by a story I'd like to tell you. It's about a boy named Ralph. His father owned the drugstore in a town where I was a frequent visitor and I knew him well. All through high school Ralph had worked in the store during his summer holidays and he became the best boy behind the soda fountain his father had ever employed.

"Trade jumps every time Ralph's here with me," the father boasted. "Not just the other boys and girls, either. Older people like to come in for a Coke and sit and joke with Ralph. He always has an answer and a grin; yet he's respectful, too. Nobody likes a cheeky kid. Ralph's not shy and he's not fresh. Folks like him.

I didn't blame the father for his partiality. The boy deserved his good opinion.

Then a change came over Ralph and the father was deeply disturbed. "I don't know what's come over him," he said. "He glowers at everybody who asks for anything, grunts when he's spoken to, or snaps out an answer that makes the other fellow sore. I'd fire him if it wasn't that he's my son. In fact, I'm going to fire him anyway."

And he did; there and then in my presence.

I was embarrassed for the father and for the son, too. Since I would be driving past his house, I offered Ralph a lift, and to my surprise, the boy accepted. This was an indication to me that he might want to talk and I decided I'd open up the subject and give him an opportunity to come out with the trouble if that was what he wanted.

"Want to spill it?" I asked when I had drawn up in front of his home and he'd made no move to get out of the car.

"I'm just a dope," he said angrily. "A dumb dope," he added.

"We all have our moments of feeling like that," I said mildly.

"Girls can drive a guy nuts," was his next explosive remark.

The story he finally told me was, I could see, something hard for a boy's pride to take. The girls had a bet among themselves as to how many sodas they could get free. One would talk to him and keep his attention while the others slipped away without paying. Or they'd keep changing their minds about their orders and then insist that he'd given them sodas when they wanted Cokes and they were only going to pay for Cokes.

"I'll bet I owe the cash register a ten-dollar bill," he said morosely. "And the only way I could figure to stop the racket was to act like such a grump they wouldn't come in."

"What did your father say when you told him?" I asked.

"I haven't told him," the boy exclaimed. "Think I want him to know he's got such a dope for a son?"

"Tell him," I advised. "And ask him to take the ten dollars out of your pay. Then," trying to improvise a way out of his dilemma for him I suggested, "keep a pocket full of quarters. And every time a girl diddles you out of a drink, let her see you take a quarter out of your own pocket and ring it up. And say to her, 'You're welcome.' She won't think it's so much fun when she knows she's costing you money."

"You don't know girls very well, do you?" he said. But I was glad to see a grin had come back to his face.

He did tell his father. Somehow the difficulty of confession had been dealt with after he'd told me the story. And between them they figured out a way to deal with the cheating girls. Ralph made a notation of every such evasion and the father charged them up against the family's account. Evidently the girls' fathers knew how to deal with daughters who did not pay for their sodas out of their own allowances.

Faults, serious and minor, are best dealt with by frankness. If you've got yourself into some sort of trouble, confess to someone who will understand and can help you work it out right. If it's a school paper you didn't write, a home chore you evaded, confess. Make it up. Take your punishment, if it is a matter of punishment, and make the lapse good if that is possible. Then you'll be able to live with yourself. Discouragement, gloom, bad temper, are often no more than the result of a guilt feeling.

A boy came to see me who was in serious trouble. Somehow he had got mixed up with a gang and, too late, found himself involved in their activities that bordered on the criminal.

"It was a plan to rob a store, just for the H—— of it," he told me miserably. "It just happened that we didn't steal anything. But what about next time?"

Gradually I won from him a complete avowal of the various smaller sins that had led him on into association with this wilder element in the school he attended.

"Is that all?" I asked at last. "Have you confessed all the wrongs you have committed?" Well, some more came out about girls and liquor and lies but finally he said, "That's the story, Dr. Peale, I spilled it all."

I shall never forget the manner in which he reacted. He stood upright and stretched. He stood on tiptoe, reaching with his fingers towards the ceiling. Then he took a deep breath. "My," he said, "I feel good!" It was an expression of release and relief. I suggested that he pray and ask God to forgive him and to fill him with peace and cleanness.

"Do you mean for me to pray aloud?" he asked dubiously. "I never did that in my life."

"Yes," I said, "it is good practice and will strengthen you."

It was a simple prayer, as I recall it. He said, "Dear Lord, I am sorry for the wrong I have done. I've told Dr. Peale all about it. Now I ask You to forgive me and to fill me with peace. Also make me strong so that I can break away from those guys. Help me to be better—lots better."

I never heard of that boy being in trouble again. He broke off his association with that crowd and it was well that he did for one by one they all got into grave difficulty.

"Honest confession is good for the soul." We've heard that all our lives. But here's one we haven't heard so much about. Honest confession is also good for the body. A physician actually told me that a man whom we both knew had died of what he called "grudgitis." He said the man had actually died as a result of a long-held hatred. "He did his body such damage with that hatred that his resistance was lowered," was what the doctor said in explanation, did not possess the stamina to overcome it. He had "so that when a physical malady attacked him he undermined himself physically by the malignancy of his illwill."

Every thoughtful person who has ever considered the matter realises that the doctors are right when they tell us that resentment, hate, grudge, illwill, jealousy, vindictiveness are attitudes which produce ill health. Have a fit of anger and experience for yourself that sinking feeling in the pit of your stomach, that sense of stomach sickness. Chemical reactions in the body are set up by emotional outbursts that result in feelings of ill health. Should these be continued either violently or in a simmering state over a period of time, the general condition of the body will deteriorate.

Dr. Charles Miner Cooper, San Francisco physician, once said, "You must curb your emotional reactions. . . . I have known a patient's blood pressure to jump sixty points almost instantaneously in response to an outburst of anger. . . . Whenever a problem starts to vex you or you begin to get angry, let yourself go limp all over. This will dissipate your mounting inner turmoil."

So I suggest if you feel low, do a job of self-analysis. Ask yourself honestly if you are harbouring any resentments or grudges. If you are, get rid of them. They don't harm the person against whom you are holding them, but they are eating at you. Many a person is upset by something he has eaten. But often the trouble isn't what you have eaten but what's eating you. Emotional ills sap your energy, reduce your efficiency, and siphon off your happiness. A person can make himself ill by resentment: he can develop various physical symptoms because of a sense of guilt, or as a result of fear or anxiety. And often healing can be accomplished only by a change in the thoughts.

Recently I was told about a girl who was admitted to the hospital with a temperature of 102 degrees. She had a definite case of rheumatoid arthritis; her joints were badly swollen.

In order to study the case thoroughly the doctor gave her no medication except a slight sedative. After two days the young woman asked the doctor, "How long will I be in this condition, and how long must I remain in the hospital?"

"I think I must tell you," replied the physician, "that you will probably be in the hospital for about six months."

"You mean it will be six months before I can get married?" she demanded.

"I am sorry," he said, "but I cannot promise you anything better."

This conversation took place in the evening. The next morning the patient's temperature was normal and the swelling was gone from her joints. Unable to account for the change, the doctor observed her for a few days, then sent her home.

In a month she was back in the hospital in the same condition as before: temperature 102, joints swollen. Counselling disclosed that her father insisted that she marry a certain man who would be an asset to him in his business. The girl loved her father, but did not want to marry a man whom she did not love. So her subconscious mind came to her assistance and in effect gave her rheumatoid arthritis.

The doctor explained to the father that if he forced this marriage his daughter could become an invalid. When told that she need not go through with the marriage, the girl's recovery was quick and permanent.

Do not get the idea that you'll get arthritis if you marry the wrong person! This incident merely illustrates the profound effect of mental pain on physical conditions.

That there is even a relationship between emotional disturbance and the common cold is indicated by Dr. L. J. Saul of the University of Pennsylvania Medical School.

"Emotional disturbances are believed to affect the blood circulation in the linings of the nose and throat. They also affect glandular secretions. These factors make the mucous membranes more susceptible to attack by cold viruses or germ infection."

Dr. Edmund P. Fowler, Jr., of Columbia University's College of Physicians and Surgeons, stated: "There are colds which develop in students at the time of their examinations and colds which develop in many persons before or after a trip. Colds develop in housewives when they must care for a large family. And one often sees a cold develop in a patient when his mother-in-law comes to live in the house, and it often disappears when she leaves." (Dr. Fowler does not specify the effects of the mother-in-law on a daughter-in-law.)

One of the cases Dr. Fowler reports concerned a twenty-five-year-old salesgirl. When she visited his office her nose was stuffy, the lining was red and congested, and she suffered from a headache and mild temperature. These symptoms had persisted for nearly two weeks. Questioning disclosed that they had started a few hours after a violent quarrel with her fiancé.

Local treatments cleared up the cold but the young woman was back in a few weeks with another attack. This time the trouble had started after an argument with the butcher. Again local treatments brought relief. But the girl continued to have recurring colds, and each time they were traced to a fit of anger. Finally Dr. Fowler was able to persuade the girl that her bad temper was at the root of her chronic symptoms. When she learned to lead a calmer existence, her sneezes and sniffles disappeared.

And yet people still think that when the Bible tells you not to hate or to get angry that it is "theoretical advice." The Bible is not theoretical. It is our greatest book of wisdom. It is filled with practical advice on living and on health. Anger, resentment, and guilt make you sick, modern physicians tell us, which proves once again that the most up-to-date book on personal well-being is the Holy Bible.

No wonder more copies are read than all other books. That is because in this book we discover not only what is wrong with us but how to correct it as well.

Dr. Fowler calls attention to "emotional colds" suffered by young people. He reports that many cases of chronic colds occur in girls and boys who come from broken homes. An older child often has recurring respiratory infection when a new baby is born because he feels neglected and jealous. For a nine-year-old boy the conflict between the strictness of one parent and the lenience of the other obviously was disturbing. He particularly feared punishment by his father. This boy suffered for several years from continuous coughs and sniffles. The colds disappeared when he went to camp—away from his parents.

Since irritation, anger, hate and resentments have such a powerful effect in producing ill health, what is the cure? Obviously to fill the mind with goodwill, forgiveness, faith, love. How is this accomplished? By following some practical suggestions.

1. Remember that anger is an emotion and an emotion is always warm, even hot. Therefore, cool it. How? Notice that when you are angry you clench your fists, your voice rises, your muscles become tense. Really you are poised to fight: this is a caveman hangover in the nervous system. So, deliberately, unclench your hands, speak in a lower tone of

voice—even reduce it to a whisper if necessary. It is difficult to quarrel in a whisper.

2. Say aloud to yourself, "This won't get me anywhere: skip it." It may be hard at the moment to pray but try it, anyway; conjure up a picture of Jesus in your mind. You can't imagine Him as being as angry as you are. This effort will puncture your mood.

3. Grace Oursler suggests the first ten words of the Lord's Prayer, "Our Father who art in Heaven, hallowed be Thy name." She says it works better than counting ten.

4. Anger is often an accumulation of a multitude of minor irritations. Therefore try to check them; see how silly each of them is. Make a list of them. By drying up these rivulets you will keep them from feeding a river of anger.

5. Make each separate irritation a special object of prayer. Get victory over each, one at a time. Snip away by prayer the little annoyances. In this way you will weaken your anger to the point where you will gain control over it.

6. Train yourself, when you feel yourself getting angry, to say, "Is it worth it? I'll only make a fool of myself. I will lose friends. Why spend a mass of emotion on a paltry irritation?"

7. When a hurt-feeling situation arises, get it straightened out as quickly as possible. Don't brood over it for a minute longer than you can help. Do something about it. Don't allow yourself to sulk or

indulge in self-pity. Do as you would do to a hurt finger—immediately apply a cure. Unless you do, the situation can become distorted out of all proportion. Put some spiritual iodine on the hurt; and say a prayer of loving forgiveness.

8. Open your mind and let grievances flow out: that is, go to someone you trust and pour it all out. Don't let a vestige of it remain. Then forget it.

9. Start praying for the person who has hurt your feelings. Continue this until you feel all the malice fading away. Sometimes you may have to pray quite a while before getting this result. But it will work.

10. Say this prayer: "May the love of Christ for [insert the name] flood my soul." Pray this and mean it; you will get relief.

11. Actually take the advice of Jesus to forgive seventy times seven. That means literally four hundred and ninety times. Before you have forgiven a person that many times you will be free of resentment.

12. Finally, your emotions can be tamed only by allowing Jesus Christ to take control. So complete this lesson by saying this prayer: "Even as You can convert a person's morals, so now I ask You to convert my nerves. Bring my temper under Your control. Give me Thy healing peace in my nervous system as well as in my soul."

CHAPTER 11

You Are What You Think

You are what you think. That is one of the most important facts about yourself. You've heard of the psychologist William James? He was one of the wisest men America every produced. In a period when men were discovering the marvels of science, he said something I hope you will never forget. He said, "The greatest discovery of my generation is that *human beings can alter their lives by altering their attitudes of mind.*"

So get rid of your worn-out thoughts, if you don't like the kind of person you are. Fill your minds with fresh, new, creative thoughts—thoughts of faith and kindness and generosity. Get rid of negative thoughts. Become a positive thinker. Do this and you'll re-make yourself.

I know some young people who are always happy and because of that characteristic they interested me so much that one day I asked one of them her secret. She was on her knees in the family vegetable garden, weeding strawberries; and she sat back on her heels —willing enough to be interrupted—and grinned at me.

"You're a minister," she said, "you ought to know."

I agreed about being a minister but I still wanted her to tell me why she could whistle while weeding strawberries, not a particularly inspiring job as anybody can testify who has ever tried it.

"Mother has always made me commit to memory whatever Bible verse we chose for the day's motto. It's an old family custom"—and she laughed. "We have quite a lot of fun, Mother and Father and Walter and I, each of us coming up with a different text.

"The idea is to use that verse all day. Whenever I have something to do that's hard, or I don't like, I recite the verse all the time I'm doing it. This morning we chose the hymn, 'Brighten the corner where you are.' That's the song I'm whistling and you must admit"—looking complacently upon the neat job of weeding she was doing—"that this corner is a lot brighter because I'm here."

Later this same girl told me that her spiritual thinking had given her a feeling of inner joy and had made things go well.

I think if you'll do a similar job of research on your friends, picking the happiest ones you know, you'll find Christianity at the root of that disposition; not formal Christianity perhaps, but at least the Christian principles of kindness and generosity in their thinking. In other words: to be happy, think happy thoughts.

I knew one such man and I persuaded him—for he is very modest—to tell me about his business methods. I knew that his plant was modern in its equipment and that a spirit of goodwill pervaded the organisation. His experience shows that a person or a business is made from how one thinks.

"That Book," he said, pointing to an old, battered copy of the Bible, "is the most up-to-date thing in this plant. Equipment wears out but that Book is so far ahead of us that it never gets out of date."

As with many people, once you get them started talking it is easy to keep them going. "My mother gave me that Bible when I went away to college," he continued without prodding. "I took it, but I thought I didn't need it. I was a dope. I got my life into a terrific mess. Everything went wrong until I discovered that it was I who was wrong. I failed at everything until I came to realise that my principal trouble was wrong thinking. I was cocky; nobody could tell me anything. I griped about everything and everybody. Nobody liked me.

"One night I came across this Bible under a mass of papers. I got to thinking about my mother and as I did I leafed the book through and I came upon a sentence that seemed meant for me."

"What was the sentence?" I asked, for he acted as if he had finished the story.

"It was at the opening of the 27th Psalm," he said. " 'The Lord is the strength of my life . . . in this will I be confident.' I don't know why that one affected me so, but it did. I decided to put my faith in God, and as I did, I began to get hold of a new set of thoughts. I began definitely to think in a new and creative way based on faith."

Do you see what I mean? You can think your way out of failure and unhappiness. You can think your way to success and happiness. Your life is not primarily determined by outward conditions and circumstances but by the thoughts that habitually occupy your mind. A modern psychologist has said, "There is a deep tendency in human nature to become precisely like that which you habitually imagine yourself to be." The chief thing about a human being is an area in the head called the mind. Actually your body is only for the purposes of carrying the mind around. In the thoughts that are generated in the mind is your whole life. Marcus Aurelius, wisest man of the Roman Empire, said, "A man's life is what his thoughts make of it"; and Emerson, a very wise American, said, "A man is what he thinks about all day long."

Thoughts have power. Actually you can think yourself into or out of situations. You can make yourself ill with your thoughts; you can make yourself well. Ask your doctor if this isn't so, at least to a limited degree. Positive thoughts create around you an atmosphere in which positive developments may live. To change something which is working against you, start thinking differently. Do not accept unhappy circumstances; instead form a picture in your mind of circumstances as they should be. Hold firmly to that picture. Believe in it; pray about it;

work at it to bring it to pass. This is one of the greatest laws of the universe. It is, in three words, *believe and succeed.*

I learned this law in a very interesting manner.

I was connected with an organisation that was trying to get a project started: a very worthwhile project, we thought. But we kept running out of money. We invited to a staff meeting a woman who had formerly helped us out of a critical need and we hoped that lightning would strike twice.

She listened to our recital of assets and obligations and plans for expansion, for which we didn't have the funds. "I suppose you gentlemen would like me to give you another financial contribution," she said drily. "I might as well put you out of your misery. I'm not going to give you a cent. If I did, you would only go in deeper. But I'll give you something far more valuable than money."

We didn't believe anything could be more valuable than money at the moment.

"I'm going to give you an idea," she said.

"How can we pay our bills with an idea?" we asked glumly.

Of course that is where we were wrong. An idea is just what helps pay bills. Every successful achievement in this world was originally an idea. One must, first, get the idea; then have faith in it; and then find the means of putting the idea into operation. That is the way to success.

"Here is the idea," she said. "What is your present

trouble? *Lack!* You *lack* everything: money, equipment, ideas, courage. Simply because you are thinking *lack*. By this constant mental emphasis on *lack* you have frustrated your creative forces. You have failed to do the one all-important thing that will lend power to your efforts. You have not employed positive thinking."

She was right, of course. We had not been demonstrating faith. We had been demonstrating lack and as a result getting lack. We began to visualise. We decided on what we needed most for success; and each of us carried a mental picture of that as happening, carried it persistently until it actually did happen.

This is a true story. The ultimate success of our enterprise has awed me. Through this experience I had stumbled on a law which I decided to apply thereafter to my own personal problems. And it works. Whenever I have failed to use this law, I have missed great results. When I have used it, things instead of going wrong have gone right in an amazing way.

It is as simple as this—put your problem in God's hands. In your thoughts rise above the problem, so that you look down upon it, not up at it. Test it according to God's will. That is, do not try to get success from something that is wrong. Be sure it is right morally, spiritually and ethically. You can never get a right result from an error. If your thinking is wrong, it is wrong and not right and can never be right so long as it is wrong. If it is wrong in the essence, it is bound to be wrong in the result.

Therefore be sure it is right, then hold it up in God's name and visualise a great result. Keep the idea of prosperity, of achievement, and of attainment firmly fixed in your mind. Never entertain a failure thought. Should a negative thought of defeat come into your mind, expel it by increasing the positive affirmation. Affirm aloud, "God is now giving me success. He is now giving me attainment." The mental vision which you create and firmly hold in consciousness will be actualised if you continually affirm it in your thoughts and if you work diligently and effectively. This creative process simply stated is: visualise, prayerise, and finally actualise.

People in all walks of life who accomplish notable achievements know the value of this law in their experience.

Henry J. Kaiser, the automobile manufacturer, told me that at one time, when an engineer, he was building a levee along a riverbank, and there came a great storm and flood which buried all his earth-moving machinery and destroyed the work that had been done. Upon going out to observe the damage after the water receded, he found his workers standing around glumly looking at the mud and buried machinery.

He came among them and said with a smile, "Why are you so glum?"

"Don't you see what has happened?" they asked. "Our machinery is covered with mud."

"What mud?" he asked brightly.

"What mud!" they repeated in astonishment. "Look around you. It is a sea of mud."

"Oh," he laughed, "I don't see any mud."

"But how can you say that?" they asked him.

"Because," said Mr. Kaiser, "I am looking up at a clear blue sky, and there is no mud up there. There is only sunshine, and I never saw any mud that could stand against sunshine. Soon it will be dried up, and then you will be able to move your machinery and start all over again."

How right he is. If your eyes are looking down in the mud and you feel a sense of failure, you will create defeat for yourself.

Another friend of mine who has been an outstanding success explains it this way: "I've had wonderful people to work with and the United States of America gives any boy unlimited opportunities. It all lies in how you think about your problems. I put all the mental power I have upon a problem; I pray about it sincerely; I ask myself what is the right thing to do. Because nothing will be right if it is wrong. Then I give it all I've got."

There is a primary, basic technique for success. Believe in the job and in yourself; pray; expect the best and give it all you've got.

At this very minute, as you read this book, potential ideas are in your mind. By releasing and developing these ideas you can attain success in your ventures. A steady inflow and practical use of these creative thoughts can re-make your life and you along with it.

There was a time when I acquiesced in the silly idea that there is no relationship between faith and prosperity; that when one talked about religion he should never relate it to achievement, that it dealt only with ethics and morals or social values. But now I realise that such a viewpoint limits the power of God and the development of the individual. Religion teaches that there is a tremendous power in the universe and that this power can dwell in personality. It is a power that can blast out all defeat and lift a person above all difficult situations.

We have seen the demonstration of atomic energy. We know that astonishing and enormous energy exists in the universe. This same force of energy is resident in the human mind. Nothing on earth is greater than the human mind in potential power. The average individual is capable of much greater achievement than he has ever realised.

This is true regardless of who is reading this statement. When you actually learn to release yourself through faith, prayer, right thinking and God's power, you will discover that your mind contains ideas of such creative value that you need not lack anything. By the full and proper use of your power stimulated by God power, you can make your life successful.

You can make just about anything of your life—anything you will believe or will visualise, anything you will pray for and work for. Look deeply into your mind. Amazing wonders are there.

Whatever your situation may be, you can improve it. First, quiet your mind so that inspirations may rise from its depths. Believe that God is now helping you. Visualise achievement. Organise your life on a spiritual basis so that God's principles work within you. Hold firmly in your mind a picture not of failure but of success. Do these things and creative thoughts will flow freely from your mind. This is an amazing law, one that can change anybody's life including your own. An inflow of new thoughts can re-make you regardless of every difficulty you may now face, and I repeat—*every difficulty*.

The basic reason a person fails to live a creative and successful life is because of error within himself. He thinks wrongly. He needs to correct the error in his thoughts. He needs to practise right thinking. When the 23rd Psalm says, "He leadeth me in the paths of righteousness," it not only means the paths of goodness, but the paths of right-mindedness as well. When Isaiah says, "Let the wicked forsake his way, and the unrighteousness man his thoughts" (Isaiah 55:7), it not only means that a person is to depart from evil and do good, but that he is to change his thinking from wrong to right, from error to truth. The great secret of successful living is to reduce the amount of error in oneself and increase the amount of truth. An inflow of new, right, health-laden thoughts through the mind creatively affects the circumstances of life, for truth always produces right procedures and therefore right results.

I know a young man who has a delightful personality, but he was at one time failing at everything. A person would employ him and be enthusiastic about him, but soon enthusiasm would cool and it was not long until the boy was out of a position. In addition to being a failure as an employee, he was a failure as a person as well. He missed connections with everything. He just couldn't do anything right and asked me, "Why is it that everything goes wrong for me?"

Still he had a lot of conceit. He was smug and had the irritating habit of blaming everybody but himself. Something it seemed was "wrong" with every office with which he was connected. He blamed everybody else for his failures—never himself. He would never look inside himself. It never occurred to him that anything could actually be wrong with him.

One night I had to make a drive of about a hundred miles to deliver a speech and he drove me there and back. On our return we stopped along about midnight at a roadside stand for a hamburger and a cup of coffee. I don't know what was in that hamburger but ever since I have had a new respect for hamburgers. For between bites he shouted, "I've got it! I've got it!"

"You've got what?" I asked in astonishment.

"I've got the answer. Now I know what's the trouble with me. It's that everything goes wrong with me because I myself am wrong."

I clapped my hand on his back and said, "Boy, at last you are on your way."

"Why, it's as clear as a crystal," he said. "I have been thinking wrong, and as a result I have created my own wrong outcomes."

By this time we were standing alongside the car, and I said to him, "Harry, you must go one step further and ask God to make you right inwardly." I quoted this passage from the Bible: " 'Ye shall know the truth, and the truth shall make you free.' (John 8: 32) Get the truth into your mind and you will be free of your failures."

He became an enthusiastic practising follower of Jesus Christ. Through real faith and a complete change of thoughts and personal habits, wrong thinking and wrong acting were removed from his nature. When he became right, then everything began to go right for him.

Following are seven practical steps for changing your mental attitudes from negative to positive; for releasing creative new thoughts; and for shifting from a pattern of thinking that brings failure to a pattern of thought that brings success.

1. For the next twenty-four hours, deliberately speak hopefully about everything: about your work

at school, about your home problems, about your friends, about your future. I realise this will be difficult. If your habit has been to talk pessimistically, or if your usual associates are those who expect the worst and say so, it will take an effort of will to change the pattern. But try it. You'll be surprised!

2. Having succeeded in establishing for yourself the hopeful pattern for twenty-four hours, give yourself the task of continuing the practice for a week.

After you have done this for a week you won't be so inclined to pessimism; things will have a more hopeful outlook. You will be making progress in the power of positive thinking.

3. You must feed your mind even as you feed your body. You eat wholesome food in order to have a healthy body. You must give your mind nourishing thoughts in order to have a healthy mental outlook on life. Start at the beginning of the New Testament. Take a page at a time and underline, or copy off on a card, every sentence that has in it the word "faith." Particularly note Mark 11: verses 22, 23, 24. Commit them to memory and repeat them frequently—several times every day. In that way they will sink deep into your consciousness and will of themselves come into your mind for use when you need them. It is needless to say, of course, that Jesus was not talking about a literal "mountain" but about the mountains of trouble with which we are all beset at times.

4. Commit to memory all the underscored pas-

sages. This will take time, of course, but how could you spend your time to greater advantage? When your mind is full of such powerful thoughts your subconscious mind will become of that character and nothing can defeat you ever.

5. Make a list of your friends and decide to cultivate the ones among them who are optimistic, positive; rather than pessimistic, negative. Do not abandon your negative friends; they need you and you may be able in time to win them to your side. But see more of the positive ones until you become so positive yourself that negative people can no longer affect you.

6. Avoid argument. But when you are drawn into a discussion, express optimistic rather than pessimistic opinions. If the other fellow wants to postpone some expedition because it might rain, you suggest that you go through with it because it might be fair weather.

7. Pray a great deal. Pray as you are walking about the house, or on the way to school—in fact in any spare moments. Keep your mind occupied with prayer; that is one sure way to avoid negativism. Remember to thank God whenever something pleasant has happened to you, or whenever some plan has turned out as you would have it—especially since God has helped you, in answer to your request, to bring it about. It is so easy to ask for help, but so many of us forget to say "Thank you, God." God is being good to you. He will give you even greater

blessings if you believe that He will. He wants to give you great things but He cannot unless, by faith, you are willing to receive. "According to your faith be it unto you." (Matthew 9:29) That means that you will receive blessings from God *in proportion* to your faith.

8. The secret of a better and happier life is to get rid of all your old, discouraged, unhappy thoughts and fill your mind with new and positive thoughts: thoughts of goodness and success and joy. God can make your life like this if you ask Him and believe. Such thinking will re-make your life. You will become whatever you think.

CHAPTER 12

Easy Does It

ARE you familiar with the word "tension"? It may not be anything you have experienced yourself—I hope not—but I am sure you have seen your mother or your father, or perhaps a teacher, in a mood when you thought it wise to walk softly: in a mood when anything you said or did would bring wrath down upon you. It will help you to know why your parents and teachers may be tense at times. And of course now, early in life, is the time to prevent yourself from becoming a tense person.

Some people allow themselves a burst of temper as a way of "taking the heat off." It's not a wise way; it hurts them and is unfair to the one who is at the receiving end. But it *is* a way.

The problem is so important that the Royal Bank of Canada some time ago devoted its monthly letter to this problem. It wrote: "Let's Slow Down." Then it went on to say in part: "This monthly letter does not set itself up as a counsellor of mental and physical health, but it is attempting to break down a problem that bedevils every adult person in Canada." And I might add, in the United States, not only adults but many young persons as well. The bank letter went on to say: "We are victims of a mounting tension; we have difficulty in relaxing. Caught up in the rush of every day, we are not living fully. We must remember what Carlyle called 'the calm supremacy of the spirit over circumstances.' "

When a prominent banking institution calls the attention of its customers to the fact that they are missing what they really want out of life because they are the victims of tension, it is time for us to give our attention to the subject. Many young people have complained to me of tension. Too much school work, too many activities, parents and friends always "pushing" them; all this they say gets them upset and "tensed up."

One of the simplest methods for reducing tension is to practise the easy-does-it attitude. Do everything more slowly, less hectically, and without pressure. My friend Branch Rickey, famous baseball man, told me that he would not use a player no matter how well he hits, fields, or runs if he is guilty of "over-pressing." To be a successful big-league baseball player there must be a flow of easy power through every action and of course through the mind. The most effective way to hit a ball is by the easy method, where all the muscles are flexible and operating in correlated power. Try to kill the ball and you will slice it or maybe miss it altogether. This is true in golf, in baseball, in every sport.

In a World Series game many years ago, the famous Ty Cobb made baseball history. Afterward he presented the bat he had used to a friend of mine. I was permitted to take the bat in my hand, and in the spirit of the game, I struck a pose. "Ty Cobb would never have done it that way," chuckled my friend. "You're too rigid, too tense. You're obviously over-trying. You'd probably strike out."

It is beautiful to watch a great ball player at the plate. It is a study in rhythm, the ease with which he gets into his swing. This is true of all success. The people who are efficient always seem to do what they have to do easily. With a minimum of effort they release a maximum of power.

I'm a dub at golf but I like to go around with an eighteen-year-old I know who is good. I mean good. He's never anxious. There's usually a grin on his face, even while he's swinging. I've tried to copy that free and easy swing; it doesn't get me anywhere but in the rough.

"How do you do it, John?" I asked one day.

"It's easy; you ought to know," and he smiled at me shyly. "In fact, you taught me how. Before every stroke I just say, 'Easy does it,' and then I swing. You ought to try it yourself," he suggested.

He's right, you know. I believe in hard work but not in working hard. Work easily and the hard work becomes easier. Some students make awfully hard work of their studies. They fight their work in their minds, building it up as hard before they start. Or else they don't do it and it piles up. Then they feel swamped. Stop thinking how hard things are. Practise thinking you can do it. Then take it in your stride with no straining. Your mind and body will be relaxed and you will make a hit in your studies just as in a game.

One February morning I was rushing along the veranda of a Florida hotel, my hands full of mail from my office in New York. I had come to Florida on a mid-winter vacation but I couldn't seem to get out of the habit of dealing with my mail the minute it arrived.

As I hurried along I could not resist a glance in the direction of the swimming pool; it was usually deserted so early in the morning and consequently this was my favourite time for a dip.

The swimming instructor was sitting dabbling his feet in the water and he waved and shouted at me. Reluctantly I allowed myself to be tempted in his direction.

"Where are you heading, Doctor, in such a rush?" he asked. "Go get into your trunks and then come and help me practise one of the greatest arts."

"What's that?" I asked.

"An art that's passing out," he said mournfully. "Not many people know how to do it any more."

"I don't see that you're practising any art," I commented.

"Oh, yes, I am," he said. "I'm practising the art of just sittin' in the sun. It's warm-like and it smells good. It makes you feel peaceful inside. Did you ever think about the sun? It never hurries, never gets excited, it just works away and makes no noise —not any we can hear. It doesn't have any telephones to answer. Doesn't ring any bells. Just goes on a-shining. And the sun does more work in the fraction of an instant than you and I could do in a lifetime. Come along down and sit in the sun with me."

I did as he suggested: went to my room, dropped my letters on my desk, changed into my swimming trunks and went down to dabble my feet in the pool and sit in the sun.

"The sun," continued my friend, the swimming instructor, just as if the conversation had not been interrupted, "keeps the trees growing, makes the flowers bloom, gives us fruits and vegetables, makes the crops ripen, draws up water from our lakes and ponds and rivers and oceans and sends it back to us. I always feel peaceful-like when I sit and think about the sun."

So I sat and thought about the sun, too, and let it do its work on me. It sent its rays into me and gave me energy. Of course I know a lot of lazy people who have been "sittin' in the sun" all their lives and never amounted to anything. There is a difference between "sittin' " and relaxing—and just "sittin'." If you sit and relax and think about God and get yourself in tune with Him and open yourself to the flow of His power, then "sittin' " is not laziness: it is the best way to renew power. It produces driving energy, the kind of energy *you* drive, not the kind that drives you. In fact you can "sit in the sun" so to speak when you're walking the streets, washing dishes, polishing the family car. The point is to relax, and think about God and become master of the skill of "Easy Does It."

When I finally went to my room, after this session of "sittin' " followed by a quick swim, I found that I finished off my mail in no time flat. You see, my mind was quiet and I had lots more drive and mental energy than if I had got tense about my work.

The secret is to avoid hectic haste and practise peaceful thinking. The essence of the art that my friend, the swimming instructor, was talking about is to keep the tension down and to keep your emotional timing right. In this way you will perform your responsibilities on the basis of the most efficient conservation of energy.

One of the best plans I know for relaxing was suggested to me by Captain Eddie Rickenbacker. He's a very busy man but he handles his responsibilities in a way that suggests he always has reserves of power that he could use if he needed them. I found out by accident one way he does this.

I was on a television programme with him. We were making a film and the filming was delayed beyond the time we had anticipated, though we had been assured that the work could be done quickly, leaving him free for other matters on his day's schedule.

Yet the Captain, I noticed, showed no impatience

He was neither nervous nor anxious. He didn't pace up and down; he didn't put in frantic calls to his office. Instead he accepted the situation gracefully. There were a couple of old rocking-chairs at the studio, apparently intended for use on a TV set other than ours. He sat down in one of those rockers and rocked calmly and contentedly.

I had always been a great admirer of Eddie Rickenbacker so I was interested in his showing this lack of tension. "I know how busy you are," I said. "I marvel at your sitting here, so quiet and peaceful-like."

He laughed and said, "I practise what you preach. Easy does it. Come on and rock in that other chair."

I did just that, pulling the chair up beside him and relaxing in my turn. "Eddie," I said, "what's your technique for keeping calm under stress, when other people would get all flustered and in a dither?"

Because I was persistent he gave me the formula. It goes something like this. First, collapse physically. You can't have a relaxed mind in a tense body. Loosen up; think of yourself as a jellyfish. Or imagine a huge burlap bag of potatoes. Then mentally cut the end of the bag and let the potatoes rush out. Imagine yourself as the bag. It is a good way to empty tension out of your muscles.

Then drain the mind; empty it of every thought of irritation and impatience. Unless the mind is freed of these exasperations, power can't flow through. If you were watering the garden you wouldn't expect a gush of water if the hose were clogged. You have to shake the kinks out of the hose and out of the mind too. Any housewife will tell you that the vacuum cleaner won't work if the bag hasn't been emptied of yesterday's dirt.

Then, third, think spiritually. Turn the mind toward God. "Lift up your eyes unto the hills." When you are in tune with God's harmony, you will be refilled with peace.

Relax: empty the mind of worry: refill it with God. Simple, isn't it?

A doctor I know has an extraordinary trick of relaxing under pressure. I've seen him, with an office full of patients, stop suddenly, lean against his desk, and talk to God. "Look, Lord," he would say, "I am pushing myself too hard. I am getting jittery. Here I am counselling people to practise quietness; now I must practise it myself. Touch me with Your healing peace. Give me composure, strength; and conserve my nervous energy so that I can help these people who are coming in to me."

He stands there for a moment or two. Then he thanks the Lord for answering his prayer and proceeds with full and easy power to do his work.

Often in making sick calls about the city he finds himself in a traffic jam. He has a most interesting method of dealing with these delays. He shuts off his engine, slumps in his seat, puts his head back, closes his eyes—he has even been known to drop off to sleep. "I don't need to worry," he grins. "The horns behind me will honk me awake when the time comes to move."

I am told that Roger Babson, the famous statistician, frequently goes into an empty church and sits quietly. Dale Carnegie, famous writer and teacher, does the same thing. These men know the importance of guarding themselves against tension.

I encountered a friend on a train from Washington to New York one night. This man is a member of Congress and he explained that he was on his way to his district to speak at a meeting of his constituents. The particular group was hostile to him, he said, and would probably try to make things very difficult for him.

"They are American citizens and I am their representative. They have a right to meet me if they want to."

"You do not seem to be much worried about it," I commented.

"No," he answered, "if I get worried about it, then I will be upset and will not handle the situation well."

"Do you have any particular method for handling such a tense situation?" I asked.

"Oh, yes," he replied, "they will be a noisy crowd—they will try to 'throw' me, maybe even get me off base or mad. But I have my own way of handling that situation. I will breathe deeply, talk quietly, speak sincerely, be friendly and respectful, hold my temper, and trust in God to see me through."

When we were doing some construction work at my farm in Pawling, New York, I watched a workman. He was shovelling a pile of sand. Stripped to the waist, his lean and muscular body worked with precision and correlation. The shovel rose and fell in perfect rhythm. He would push the shovel into the pile, lean his body against it, and drive it deep into the sand. Then, in a clear, free swing it came up and the sand was deposited without a break in the motion. Again the shovel went back into the sand, again his body leaned against it, again the shovel lifted easily in a perfect arc. I almost had a feeling that I could sing in rhythm to the motion of this workman.

I was not surprised when the foreman told me that he was considered one of his best workmen. Here was a relaxed man who lived with joyous power, master of the art of "Easy Does It."

Relaxation results from re-creation, and the process of re-creation should be continuous. The human being is meant to be attached to a continual flow of force that proceeds from God through the individual and back to God for renewal.

Now, how to master this important skill? I am suggesting ten rules to help in learning to do everything the easy way. These suggestions will help you to relax and have easy power. For just relaxation isn't the point: the point is to make use of our maximum ability through the added strength that comes of relaxing our bodies and minds and letting God do it, through us.

1. You know the story of Atlas, don't you, in your Greek mythology? Perseus, who had slain the Gorgon, Medusa, flew far and wide, and came at night to the western limit of the earth where the sun goes down. It was the realm of King Atlas, and Perseus begged from him shelter for the night. But Atlas had been warned that a son of Jove would rob him of his golden apples. So he told Perseus to begone.

"Since you value my friendship so little," Perseus said to the giant, "deign to accept a present." And, turning his face away, he held up the Gorgon's head which he had carried in a sack. Atlas, at the sight, was turned to stone. His beard and hair became forests, his arms and shoulders cliffs, his head a summit, and his bones rocks. Each part increased in bulk until he became a mountain so that heaven with all its stars rests upon his shoulders.

Don't get the idea that you are Atlas, carrying the weight of the heavens on your shoulders. Don't strain so hard; don't take yourself so seriously.

2. Determine to like your work. Make yourself like it; you can. No matter what you are doing, studying a subject in which you aren't interested, cutting the grass for your father, going on an errand for your mother, make up your mind that it's fun. Find fun in it. It's there to find if you look for it.

Perhaps you are studying the history of Ancient Greece, and it bores you. Read all you can about those old Greeks; read their plays. Read their stories, like the one about Atlas, in your Greek mythology. And remember that those people you are studying about believed those stories were true. Try to think what life would be like if you believed these feats of gods and goddesses, of heroes and mortals. The more you know about any subject, the more interesting you will find it.

You don't like to do chores about the house and grounds? Neither do your mother and father. A lot of us have chores to do that don't interest us at all. But we can tell ourselves how necessary they are; we can imagine what things would be like if they went undone. And presently, we will find that they *are* done. And we haven't minded. Find ways to help yourself to like your work.

3. Plan your work. And then follow your plan; make it come true. Lack of planning, procrastination, doing only the things we enjoy doing and putting off until last the things we don't like to do—that's the way one gets that "swamped" feeling. Only by planning your days and following through will you come up at evening with the satisfied feeling of accomplishment. I find I'm most likely to get through with a programme of work that I have laid out for myself if I do the task I like least first. Let's say you like mathematics but hate Latin. All right. Begin with Latin. Perhaps you don't mind writing

an English theme but you have an intense aversion to French verbs. Begin your preparations for the next day's recitations with the French verbs. You will be doing the disliked thing when you are freshest, and also, with it out of the way the rest will come easier. And this is the extraordinary result that you'll discover for yourself eventually. You'll begin to like French. Because you'll always be well prepared. And the thing we do well, we like. You can trust yourself to write that English theme, since you enjoy English. So begin with French.

4. Don't try to do everything at once. You have, we'll say, four preparations for tomorrow's lessons. Forget three of them and concentrate on the one you have decided to take up first. Pretend to yourself that that is the only one you have to do; and that you don't need to hurry. You'll find your preparation will go not only better but more quickly. Because you will be giving the whole of your mind to the task; not just the fringe, while the rest of it is saying, "Oh, dear. I must hurry! I've those other three lessons to do."

Time, you know, is spread out. No two minutes occupy the same space. They come along one after the other. And one can't appear until its predecessor is out of the way. Take your time. Heed this wise advice from the Bible: "This one thing I do." (Philippians 3:13)

5. Get a correct mental attitude. Remember that the ease or the difficulty of the work ahead of you

depends on how you think about it. Make up your mind that it's going to be hard, and it will be hard. Suppose a girl's mother has left her instructions to make a cake for supper. If the girl says, "Mother knows I've never made a cake Why should she tell me to do that?" she'll probably have a difficult time of it, and I doubt if the cake will be very appetising. But suppose she says, "What fun! Mother is letting me make a cake by myself! Of course all I have to do is to follow the directions. Alice makes cakes often for her family. If Alice can, I can." Then it will be fun. I'd take a chance on eating a slice of any cake that is made in such a spirit.

Think it's going to be hard, and you make it hard. Think it's going to be easy, and you'll find it tends to be easy.

6. Become efficient at your work. As I said under section 3: the thing you learn to do well, you learn to like to do. Don't bother about thinking whether you like it or not; don't waste time trying to get out of doing it. Get down to it. And learn to do it so well that you will be proud of the result. Remember: "Knowledge is power."

7. Practise being relaxed. If the job ahead of you is something you dread, relax. If you let it make you tense, it will be twice as difficult. If it is something you hate doing and know you must do, relax. The sooner you get at it, the sooner it will be finished. Take it in your stride; start at it. The sooner you do that the sooner it will be done. Besides, when you

start it suddenly seems simple. Get on with it. And if it's something you aren't sure you are able to do, all the more will you need to relax. For you will need the extra skill that comes of "Easy Does It."

8. Discipline yourself. Life grows easier, more interesting, and we grow more efficient as we form the habit of doing what we tell ourselves to do. Don't let yourself dodge and evade the job you don't like. Do it. Get it over. Keep your work up to schedule. You've heard about Longfellow's blacksmith under the spreading chestnut tree:

> Something attempted, something done,
> Has earned a night's repose.

A person never is very proud of himself when he goes to bed at night, knowing there was something he had to do that day which he has not done. Self-discipline is very important, not only to efficiency but to personal satisfaction as well.

9. Pray about your work. And this means pray frequently, even while you're at the job. As you turn a page, say, "Please, Lord, help me to understand what I read so that I won't have to go over it again." Or, "If the answer to this problem is wrong, Lord, make me uneasy about it so I shall know it's wrong and go over the work and find the mistake." Pray all the time about everything. That is the way to develop relaxed efficiency.

10. Remember that Jesus Christ is really your "unseen partner." He's always there, eager and

ready to help. All that is needed is for you to ask Him and open your mind and heart to Him. He carries the burden. He is as much at home in the schoolroom as in the churches. He knows more about the jobs you have been given to do than you do. Take His help. It will make your work easy.

CHAPTER 13

You Like People—People Like You

EVERYONE wants people to like him. It creates an atmosphere in which he thrives. Why do young children go through the "show off" stage of development? They are trying to get people to like them. It is a basic need with you and with me. We do our best work, we are happiest, most at ease, when we are with people who like us. It is a natural and a healthy instinct, and when someone says he doesn't care whether others like him, he isn't telling the truth to you or to himself.

A poll was taken among some high school students on the question, "What do you most desire?" By overwhelming majority the students voted that they wanted to be popular. Indeed it is doubtful if anybody ever outlives the desire to be well thought of, or to have the affection of his associates.

To master the art of popularity, be artless. Strive deliberately after popularity and the chances are you will never attain it. But become one of those rare personalities about whom people say, "He certainly has something," and you can be certain you are on the way to having people like you.

I must warn you, however, that despite your attainments in popularity you will never get everybody to like you. There is a curious quirk in human nature whereby some people, perhaps a very few, just naturally won't like you. A quatrain inscribed on a wall at Oxford says:

> I do not love thee, Dr. Fell,
> The reason why I cannot tell;
> But this alone I know full well,
> I do not love thee, Dr. Fell.

That verse is very subtle. The author did not like Dr. Fell. He didn't know why but he just knew he didn't like him. Perhaps if the author had known him better he would have liked him. It may have been due simply to that baffling mechanism by which we either do or do not "click" with certain people.

Even the Bible recognises this unhappy fact about human nature, for it says, "If it be possible, as much as lieth in you, live peaceably with all men." (Romans 12:18)

The Bible advised the disciples that if they went into a village and after trying their best to get along with people still couldn't do so, they were to shake off the very dust of the village from their feet—"And whosoever will not receive you, when ye go out of that city, shake off the very dust from your feet for a testimony against them." (Luke 9:5) This is all by way of saying that you will be wise if you do not let it too seriously affect you if you do not achieve perfect popularity with everyone.

However, there are certain formulas and procedures which, if followed faithfully, can make you a person whom other people like. You can enjoy satisfactory personal relationships even if you are a "difficult" person or by nature shy and retiring, even unsocial. You can make of yourself one who enjoys easy, normal, natural and pleasing relationships with others.

I cannot urge you too strongly to consider the importance of this subject and to give time and attention to its mastery, for you will never be fully happy or successful until you do. To be liked is of profounder importance than mere ego satisfaction. As necessary as that is to your success in life, normal and satisfactory personal relations are even more important.

The feeling of not being wanted or needed is one of the most devastating of all human reactions. In the degree to which you are sought after or needed by other people will you become a fully released and developed person. The "lone wolf," the retiring individual, these people suffer a misery which is difficult to describe. In self-defence they retire even further within themselves. Unless the personality is drawn out of itself and can be of value to someone, it may sicken and die. The feeling of not being wanted or needed produces frustration, and even illness. If you have a feeling of uselessness, if nobody needs or wants you, you really ought to do something about it. It is not only a pathetic way to live but is serious psychologically. Those who deal with the problems of human nature constantly encounter this problem and its unfortunate results.

At a Rotary Club luncheon I was at the table with two physicians, father and son. The younger man, only recently taken into practice by an ageing physician in a nearby small town, rushed in looking frazzled. He slumped into his chair and exclaimed with a certain degree of self-importance, "I didn't think I'd make it."

The father said mildly, "But this is your day off, Barney. I asked you because I thought you'd like to see some of your old friends."

"Oh, I do," the young man said hastily. "But patients telephone me, even when they know it's Wednesday. I'd like to put a silencer on that instrument."

An older man at the table who had recently taken his own son into partnership in his business glanced at the youthful doctor. "I know just how you feel. I used to say that, myself. Not any more. Now my boy, young Oliver, gets all the calls. I still go down to the office. I pick up the phone when it rings. 'Mr. Selden?' a voice asks. 'Speaking,' I say. 'What can I do for you?' But the voice persists, 'Is this Mr. Selden, Junior?' So I hand the phone across the desk to the boy."

Then he said to the young doctor, "Be glad that

people want and need you. I feel completely out of it, for nobody wants or needs me."

Here's another example. A very young wife, a busy and charming person in great demand socially and civically, came to see me.

"I just don't know what to do about Mother," she said. "She's not happy. I can't give up my whole life to being with her. I have Jim, the baby, and all sorts of committees and things. I'm busy! But she's hurt if I don't go to see her every day. And when I do go she's hurt, because I can't stay to lunch or dinner or something. I don't know what to do!"

I didn't blame her. I know it is a serious problem with many young husbands and wives, young men and women in their first jobs. They have a new way of life before them, yet the old obligations cling. What is the trouble with these clinging parents? They want to be liked; they want to be as imporatnt to their children after they are grown up as they had been when they were growing.

There are duties on both sides of that fence. The parents must set their young people free, must realise that only by doing so can they be happy themselves. They must find for themselves new occupations and interests.

And the youthful independents, on their own, feeling out their powers, testing their wings, must realise that nobody is ever independent of another; that they need their parents even as the parents need them. While helping the older people to new interests and duties, they need to resist the selfish impulse to cut all bonds. Those ties are made of love, and love is life's greatest treasure.

I tried to make this clear to that young wife. I tried to show her that she would lose more than she would gain if she shoved her mother out of her life or brushed her off. Even a daily telephone call would help, a call in which she explained the day's activities, talked over her problems with her mother. It wasn't her physical presence the mother wanted, it was the feeling that the tie still held, that she could still be of importance and use to her daughter.

We all need each other. And we all need to feel needed.

A girl of twenty-one told me that she had felt unwanted and unloved ever since birth. This serious idea had sunk into her subconscious, giving her a profound sense of inferiority and self-deprecation. It made her shy and backward, even bitter, causing her to retreat into herself. She became lonely and unhappy and was, in fact, an under-developed personality. The cure for her condition was to remake her life spiritually, especially her thinking. She was given some responsibilities which made her feel useful. People took a genuine interest in her which made her feel loved and appreciated. This process in time made her a well-liked person by setting her personality free of herself.

Countless other people have never mastered the knack of being popular. They try hard enough.

They even go to extremes, often acting in a manner they do not really enjoy, but which they employ only because of their intense desire for popularity.

The fact is that popularity can never be attained in that way, but by a few simple, natural, normal and easily mastered techniques. Practise them diligently and you can become a well-liked person.

First, become a comfortable person; that is, one with whom people can associate without a sense of strain. Of some people it is said, "You can never quite get next to him." There is always a barrier that you can't get over. A comfortable person is easy-going and natural. He has a pleasant, kindly, genial way about him. Being with him is not unlike wearing an old hat or an old pair of shoes, or an easy old coat.

Some young people were talking about a seventeen-year-old boy whom they liked very much. Of him they said, "He is good company. He is a good sport. He is easy to be with." It is very important to cultivate the quality of being natural. Usually that sort of individual is large-souled. Little people who are much concerned about how you treat them, who are jealous of their place or position, who meticulously stand on their prerogatives, are stiff and easily offended.

You have heard of James A. Farley, at one time Postmaster General of the United States. I first met him a number of years ago, After several years I met him again and he called me by name. Being human,

I've liked Mr. Farley ever since. He is a great expert at getting people to like him.

And here's one of the secrets of his popularity. It's an interesting example. I went to speak at a book-and-author luncheon in Philadelphia. I didn't witness this incident, but a friend did and he told me about it. Mr. Farley and two other authors were walking along the hotel corridor together when they passed a maid standing by her cart loaded with sheets, towels—the equipment with which she was servicing the rooms. She was paying no attention to the group as they turned aside to avoid her cart. But Mr. Farley stopped, put out his hand and said, "Hello, there. How are you? I'm Jim Farley. What's your name?" And when she had told him, he repeated it and said, "Glad to see you."

I've no doubt he'll know that girl next time he sees her in that Philadelphia hotel and will call her by name and stop to talk with her. He's that kind of man.

My friend told me that the girl's smile was wide as she watched him walk away down the corridor. I know: he's a politician and it's good business to make friends with people. But he lives in New York, not in Philadelphia. He wasn't after that girl's vote. He's just a comfortable, outgoing person who loves people. That's why he's successful in personal relationships.

The psychology department in a university conducted an analysis of the personality traits of people who are liked or disliked. And it was reported that a person must have forty-six out of a possible hundreds traits in order to be liked. That's a lot of traits! Forty-six traits in order to be liked!

However, Christianity teaches that one basic trait will go a long way toward getting people to like you. That trait is an honest and sincere liking for other people. This is a trait that it is possible to cultivate. Think about the person you are with and truly esteem him. Listen to what he is saying and show an interest. Don't wait impatiently until he is through just to start talking yourself. The better you know him, the better you will like him—(or at least, if it doesn't work that way, if you find that you are liking him less and less, you'll know he's not the friend you want to seek out and cultivate).

But haven't you known people who seem to be almost holding their breath, waiting for you to stop talking so they can talk—and usually about themselves? All right; practise listening. Maybe what they have to say will interest you. Maybe, when you've listened to them, they'll listen to you. And all the time you're learning about people. You're thinking about people. That is vastly more important than making them listen to you. You already know about "you"; try to learn about them.

If others don't talk to you, don't seek you out as a listener or don't want to be with you, then you should try to make a study of your own personality to find out why. Don't take it for granted that the fault is in them. It may be, of course. But it is better to assume that it is something in you that holds them off. Find out what it is and work to get rid of it.

This is as painful as it sounds; we don't like to hunt for faults in ourselves. If you are what we call a "difficult" person, it may be that you developed that quality in the first place as a defence against something or somebody that hurt you. It is important to try to remember what that experience was. When you understand and forget it, you're not so likely to be "difficult" any more.

A man came to talk to me about this very difficulty. He was a fine-looking young fellow, and it seemed unbelievable that people shouldn't like him. Yet he assured me that such was the case. In fact I was aware of his unpopularity.

"I do my best," he explained. "I try to get along with people. But I seem to get nowhere with them. They just don't like me and I can't help knowing it."

After talking with him a while it wasn't difficult to understand the reason for the trouble. He was critical of everything and everybody. Although he didn't often come right out with criticisms, he had an unattractive habit of drawing his lips into a thin line of disapproval. He looked prim, disdainful, and as if he thought himself superior. He probably did. A sense of annoying superiority is something you'll often find in people who are otherwise likeable. They may be intelligent, they may be neat and even attractive in their dress. But if they have that attitude of thought that it is *they* who are right about everything and *you* who are wrong, you're not going to like them. Humility may be a difficult virtue to achieve, but it is a very charming one.

This young man's personality seemed to be inflexible, even rigid.

"Isn't there some way I can stop rubbing people the wrong way?" he asked.

That was quite a problem to solve. The only person that boy really liked was himself, but he wasn't having too good a time with himself. He was self-centred, egotistical. The only possible answer was that he would have to learn to love others more than himself. He would have to practise forgetting himself and thinking about other people. Since he was being unpleasant to them in his thoughts, criticising them to himself, his thinking processes would have to change radically. While he was polite enough, other persons felt a coolness and indifference in him and so they gave him the "brush-off." That was his complaint. Of course they brushed him off! He liked himself too well to be interested in them.

He was bewildered and baffled when we outlined his difficulty. But he was sincere and meant business. He really practised the suggested techniques for developing love of others in place of his self-love. It required some fundamental changes to accomplish this, but he succeeded in doing so.

One method suggested was that at night before retiring he make a list of persons he had met during the day, as for example, the bus driver or a new teacher. He was to picture mentally each person whose name appeared on the list, and as he brought each face up before him he was to think a kindly thought about that person. Then he was to pray for each one. He was to pray around his little world. Each of us has his own world, people with whom we are associated in one way or another.

Since he lived in an apartment building in New York, the first person outside the family whom this boy saw in the morning was the elevator man in his apartment house. He had not been in the habit of saying anything to him beyond a perfunctory and growled good morning. Now he took time to have a little chat with the elevator man. He found that the elevator operator had an interesting point of view and some experiences which were quite fascinating. He began to see new values in a person who to him previously had been a robot, who ran the elevator up and down to his floor. He actually began to like the elevator operator and in turn the elevator man, who had formed a pretty accurate opinion of the young man, began to revise his views. They established a friendly relationship. So the process went from person to person.

One day the boy said to me, "I have found that the world is filled with interesting people and I never realised it before."

When he made that observation he proved that he was losing himself, and when he did that, as the

Bible so wisely tells us, he found himself. In losing himself he found himself and lots of new friends besides. People learned to like him.

Learning to pray for people was important in his rehabilitation, for when you pray for anyone you tend to modify your personal attitude toward him. You lift the relationship thereby to a higher level. The best in the other person begins to flow out toward you as your best flows toward him. In the meeting of the best in each a higher unity of understanding is established.

Essentially, getting people to like you is merely the other side of liking them. One of the most popular men who lived in the United States was the late Will Rogers. One of the most characteristic statements he ever made was, "I never met a man I didn't like." That may have been a slight exaggeration, but I am sure Will Rogers did not regard it as such. That is the way he felt about people, and as a result people opened up to him like flowers to the sun.

A popular man whom I know is a Houston, Texas, philanthropist. His name is Hugh Roy Cullen. You have probably heard of him, for he has given millions of dollars to the University of Houston, to other educational institutions, to hospitals, churches, and charities.

Well, you may say, it seems easy enough to be popular if you have all that money to give away. But the point is that Mr. Cullen is not popular because of his money. It might rather be said that he has his money because of his popularity.

Of course, it took more than just popularity to be successful as an oil producer. That is a business in which there are enormous expenses, with excellent chances of losing all in dry wells. He did not have all the money he needed when he drilled his first well. What he did have was a host of friends, and the reputation that any man could rely absolutely on his word.

If he stated a fact, you knew it was true, and anyone could depend upon it. If he promised to repay a loan on a certain date, he did it, whether his plans worked out as he expected, or not. As a result, he could borrow thousands of dollars with no more collateral than his personal word, because no better security existed.

Hugh Roy Cullen's friends were glad to see him succeed. They helped him when they could, and were never envious. Now, looking back, he says he has lived a selfish life. By that he means he has taken great pleasure in giving away dollars in the hundreds of millions, because he enjoys seeing others benefit.

Sometimes the weak objection is offered that it is difficult to like some people. Granted, some people are by nature more likeable than others, nevertheless a serious attempt to know any individual will reveal qualities within him that are admirable, even lovable.

A man had the problem of conquering feelings of

irritation toward persons with whom he was associated. For some people he had developed a very profound dislike. But he conquered these feelings simply by making an exhaustive list of everything he could possibly admire about each person who annoyed him. Daily he attempted to add to this list of likeable features. He was surprised to discover that people whom he thought he did not like at all proved to have many pleasing qualities. In fact, he was at a loss to understand how he ever disliked them after becoming conscious of their attractive points. Of course, while he was making these discoveries about them, they, in turn, were finding new and likeable qualities in him.

If you have gone through life without having established satisfactory human relationships, do not assume that you cannot change; but it will be necessary to take very definite steps towards solving the problem. You can change and become a popular person if you will make the effort. May I remind you, as I remind myself, that one of the greatest tragedies of the average person is the tendency to spend his whole life perfecting his faults? We develop a fault and we nurse it and cultivate it, and never change it. Like a needle caught in the groove of a defective record on a gramophone, it plays the same old tune over and over again. You must lift the needle out of the groove, then you will have disharmony no longer. Don't spend any more of your life perfecting faults in human relations. Spend the rest of your life perfecting your great capacities for friendliness, for good personal relations are vitally important to successful living.

Another important factor in getting people to like you—and really, it comes naturally, if you have learned a genuine affection for them—is to be gentle with them. People are more sensitive than is ever apparent. One's inner personality or ego is easily hurt. Our own self-love doesn't go very deep in most of us; we don't think as well of ourselves, perhaps, as we should. So any indication that another thinks slightingly of us, our opinions, our looks or our abilities—cuts. So don't deflate another's self-respect; build it up. In that way you help the other person to be his best self. You have shown appreciation of him. Consequently he will be grateful to you and he will like you. I'm not talking about or advising insincere flattery. That gives pleasure, too, but it is harmful both to the giver and to the taker. Besides, people instinctively recognise phoney attitudes. What I mean is to understand and show genuine appreciation of that shy inner worth that lives in everybody.

Suppose a person has just told a joke or a story that you have heard before. Everybody present has been amused and the teller of the tale is pleased. That is natural. We all like to have given pleasure, even momentarily, to our fellows. But you've heard the story before. Do you have to say so? Of course you don't. You're under no obligation to tell everything you know and you'll only deflate a pleasant and friendly person. Would you do such an unkind thing to build up your own ego, your own feeling of superiority? Never do that, for if you want popularity you will have to earn it by remembering the other person's ego and forgetting your own. Build the other fellow up and in time he will do that for you.

In line with this subject of building up instead of tearing down another person's self-respect, I am reminded of an incident that has to do with a college senior and a college president.

It was a beautiful moonlight night in June and the young man of my story had just graduated. There's a thrill in that moment, but there is also sorrow and quite a bit of fright. What next? Am I going to make something of my life, or am I not? People do fail! How do I know I won't be one of them?

This college president happened to be walking across the campus with the young man. They were leaving the graduating class banquet.

"Boy," he said, putting his hand on the lad's shoulder, "I've always liked you. I've always believed in you. You have great possibilities. I know I am going to have the chance to be proud of you some day. You've got it in you."

Now, what do you imagine that did for that young man? It nerved him against future discouragements. It came back to him again and again when the going was tough. It built him up and made future accomplishment almost a "must."

I know. You see, I was that boy.

Now, of course, that president made similar statements to numberless boys and girls as they left that institution. And I am sure the result was always the same. He made them know that he loved them, respected them, approved of them. In turn, they loved him, respected him and against all odds won his subsequent commendations. They just had to prove to him that he had not been mistaken in them, and I do not doubt that every one of them had a special place in his heart for that wonderful college president.

The one whom you help to build up becomes a better and a stronger person in consequence. But you must do it unselfishly; because you like him; because you see possibilities in him.

Do this and you will never lack friends. Think well of people, and they will think well of you. Give them esteem and affection and they will give you back esteem and affection.

The basic principles of getting people to like you are very simple. They are not difficult or complicated. Anyone can master them. I am listing ten practical rules for winning the respect and regard of others. Practise them and people will like you.

1. Learn to remember names. It is a most delicate form of showing esteem and always pleases, for a

man's name is very important to him. It is the identification of his ego. Learning and remembering names can be mastered. Listen carefully when the name is given; try to associate it with the face of the person so that one calls up the other in your mind. Rehearse it to yourself after the meeting; concentrate on the person, remembering the face, repeating the name.

2. Be a comfortable sort of person; someone whom it is easy to meet, easy to talk to, pleasant to see again; in other words an "old shoe" sort of person.

3. Be relaxed. If you have learned to be an easy-going sort of person whom nothing upsets, then people are going to like seeing you, being with you.

4. Don't pet your own ego; pet the other fellow's instead. Don't think you know it all. Learn to be humble.

5. Be an interesting person from whom other people get something of value. That means read a lot; talk with people who know something you don't know; get about. And keep your mind open. Listen more than you talk. And always remember that to be interesting you must be interested.

6. Don't be "scratchy" or "difficult." A person who is irritable isn't a pleasant person. Nobody wants to associate with him.

7. Don't let misunderstanding grow. With honest Christian love in your heart, try to come to terms with anybody with whom you have had trouble.

Forget your grievances. Don't carry them in your heart.

8. Practise liking people. If you keep at it, you will make it true. Try to be like Will Rogers who was able to say, "I never met a man I didn't like."

9. Never miss an opportunity to congratulate another on his achievements, or on his good fortune. Remember always to express sympathy when he has cause for grief. Share others' good and bad days. Practise real spiritual fellowship with people.

10. And this is the most important of all. Get a deep spiritual experience. Get God into your heart and life. When you know God you have something to give other people that is priceless. With Him and His help, you can help them.

Give love to people, and you will give them strength. And they in turn will give you affection.

It's really easy to get people to like you. You have only to like them.

CHAPTER 14

Why Not Use That Higher Power?

FOUR boys were gathered, as college students do, in the room of two of them. They had been talking over everything: girls, games, and even classroom problems. They all knew that one of them, due to a football accident, was facing an operation on his knee that might mean permanent lameness. And the boy, though he tried to hide it, was in a panic. It seemed to him, and he frankly said so, that life wouldn't be worth living if he had to limp through it.

"Sid," said one of them as he was leaving, hesitant and shy as any boy would be, "I'd like to suggest something. Don't think I'm preaching. But it's what pulled me through last spring when there was that trouble at home about my sister."

All the boys avoided looking at the one who was speaking. It had been serious trouble as they knew; but it had come out all right. The girl had come to see her folly and had broken off with the older, married man with whom she was becoming involved. It was the sort of thing a fellow's friends don't talk about to him.

"It really works," the young man said. "Why don't

you draw upon that Higher Power?" Then he left the room abruptly.

"I know what he means," the boy Sid said to his room-mate later. "And he's right. I'm being a cowardly sort of pup. I'll do what Bob did: I'll pray myself through this spot."

He did; and the operation was successful. The boy was not lamed; he even was allowed back on the football team the following season.

That is advice we all need, every single one of us. We're all of us up against problems every day of our lives. We may be depressed and unhappy. We may be only puzzled and uncertain. But we are in need of hclp and the kind of guidance that comes only from that Higher Power. There isn't a day—why, there isn't even an hour—of our lives when we don't need Him. Why don't we draw upon that Higher Power which is ours for the asking? We don't doubt God, do we? Perhaps we are reluctant to pay the price, to give up our selfish wish for our own way. But it's worth it. The peace and happiness that come as a result of giving God the direction of our lives is worth it. And in the end, surprisingly, we find there has been nothing we had to give up that has any great value; we even cease to want what we thought was so precious. So try that Higher Power.

Let me tell you about a personal experience. When quite young, I was called to be the pastor of a large church in a university community and many of my congregation were professors in the university as well as leading citizens of the city. I wanted to justify the confidence of those who gave me such an outstanding opportunity at such a youthful age and accordingly worked very hard. As a result I began to experience over-strain. Everyone should work hard, but there is no virtue in over-trying to such an extent that you do not work efficiently. It is somewhat like making a golf shot. Try to "kill" the ball and you execute the shot poorly. You can do likewise in your job. I began to get rather tired and nervous and had no feeling of normal power.

One day I decided to call on one of the professors, the late Hugh M. Tilroe, a great friend of mine. He was a wonderful teacher, and he was also a great fisherman and hunter. He was a man's man, an outdoor personality. I knew that if I did not find him at the university he would be out on the lake fishing; and sure enough, there he was. He came ashore at my hail. "The fish are biting—come on," he said. I climbed into his boat and we fished awhile.

"What's the matter, son?" he asked with understanding. I told him how hard I was trying and that it was getting me down nervously. "I have no feeling of lift or power," I said.

He chuckled. "Maybe you're trying too hard."

As the boat scraped the shore he said, "Come into the house with me." When we entered his cabin he ordered, "Lie down there on that couch. I want to read you something. Shut your eyes and relax while I find the quotation."

I did as directed, and thought he was going to read me some philosophical or perhaps diverting piece, but instead he said, "Here it is. Listen quietly while I read it to you. And let these words sink in. 'Hast thou not known? Hast thou not heard, that the everlasting God, the Lord, the Creator of the ends of the earth, fainteth not, neither is weary? There is no searching of his understanding. He giveth power to the faint; and to them that have no might he increaseth strength. Even the youths shall faint and be weary, and the young men shall utterly fall: But they that wait upon the Lord shall renew their strength; they shall mount up with wings as eagles; they shall run, and not be weary; and they shall walk, and not faint.' " (Isaiah 40:28–31) Then he asked, "Do you know from what I am reading?"

"Yes, the fortieth chapter of Isaiah," I answered.

"I'm glad you know your Bible," he commented. "Why don't you practise it? Now relax. Take three deep breaths—in and out slowly. Practise resting yourself in God. Practise depending upon Him for His support and power. Believe He is giving it to you now and don't get out of touch with that power. Yield yourself to it—let it flow through you.

"Give your job all you've got. Of course you must do that. But do it in a relaxed and easy manner like a batter in a big-league ball game. He swings the bat easy-like, and doesn't try to knock the ball out of the park. He just does the best he can and believes in himself because he knows that he has lots of reserve power." Then he repeated the passage again: " 'They that wait upon the Lord shall renew their strength.' "

That was a long time ago, but I never forgot that lesson. He taught me how to draw upon that Higher Power, and believe me, his suggestions worked. I continued to follow my friend's advice, and it has never failed me in the more than twenty years that have passed since then. My life is crowded with activity but that power formula gives me all the strength I need.

A friend of mine who was once a pitcher for the New York Yankees, then the Chicago Cubs and finally the Cincinnati Reds, always drew upon the Higher Power. Once he pitched a game when the temperature was over one hundred degrees. He lost several pounds as a result of the afternoon's exertion. At one stage of the game his energy sagged. His method for restoring his ebbing strength was unique. He simply repeated that same passage from the Old Testament—"But they that wait upon the Lord shall renew their strength; they shall mount up with wings as eagles; they shall run, and not be weary; and they shall walk, and not faint."

The pitcher who had this experience told me that reciting this verse on the pitcher's mound actually gave him a renewal of strength so that he was able to complete the game with energy to spare. He explained the technique by saying, "I passed a powerful energy-producing thought through my mind."

This same pitcher never went on to the diamond that he did not believe the Lord was there to help him, not necessarily to win but to be at his best. I know two other big-league players who pray while the National Anthem is being played at the opening of a game and who draw help from God.

A second method for drawing upon that Higher Power is to learn to take a positive, optimistic attitude toward every problem. In direct proportion to the intensity of the faith which you muster will you receive power to meet your situations. "According to your faith be it unto you" (Matthew 9:29) is a basic law of successful living.

There is a Higher Power, and that Power can do everything for you. Draw upon it and experience its great helpfulness. Why be defeated when you are free to draw upon that Higher Power? State your problem. Ask for a specific answer. Believe that you are getting that answer. Believe that now, through God's help, you are gaining power over your difficulty.

This Higher Power is one of the most amazing facts in human existence. I am awestruck, no matter how many times I have seen the phenomenon, by the thorough-going, tremendous, overwhelming changes for good that it accomplishes in the lives of people. Personally, I am so enthusiastic about all that the Higher Power can do for people that I am loath to bring this book to a close. I could recite story after story about people of all ages—youngsters like you who are reading this—incident after incident of those who have laid hold of this power.

This power is constantly available. If you open to it, it will rush in like a mighty tide. It is there for anybody under any circumstances or in any condition. This tremendous inflow of power is of such force that in its inrush it drives everything before it, casting out fear, hate, sickness, weakness, moral defeat, scattering them as though they had never touched you, refreshing and re-strengthening your life with health, happiness, and goodness.

Shall we recapitulate? Let's go back over the principles of positive thinking and techniques of successful living which have been outlined.

In Chapter 1, I have tried to encourage you to rust yourself. No stream rises higher than its source. A person who believes himself predoomed to failure s just going to fail. If a man says, "I'd like to do more for my family, but I haven't any ability, I'm not worth any more than I'm being paid,"—well, he ust isn't worth any more, and he hasn't the ability o do better. But he could be. Nobody knows his own capabilities. But God knows. Nobody can fully elease that greater power and skill that is within him; but God can. You may not amount to much on our own. But *you plus God* are a power the extent f which can't be measured.

You're "dumb," you say. You can't do your lessons? Don't be silly. Of course you can do your lessons, if you open your mind and let God in. He'll prove to you that you can actually lead your class. Can you imagine God at the bottom of the class? You get into partnership with God and you will go up to the top with Him.

You're so slow on your feet that you can't make the second team, to say nothing of the first? That's foolish talk. Muscular co-ordination is something God can give you. Stop talking yourself down to yourself. Say to yourself, "God's catching that ball for me," and then—catch it, God and you together.

The secret, as I said in the beginning, is to fill your mind with thoughts of faith, of self-confidence, of security. These thoughts will force out doubt. With God all things are possible.

In Chapter 2 we were talking about peace of mind. No mind in a turmoil can be a God-filled mind. When your mind is clean; when you have driven from it all unkind thoughts, all resentments all ideas of getting even, all ideas of getting by and evading duties, all thoughts that you wouldn't want others to see if your mind were open for inspection —only then can God get in. He's willing. He's waiting. But you have to sweep and dust and clean and polish to get ready for Him. And when you are clean, and have asked Him in, and He takes over the feeling of peace that will come over you will be indescribable. And the surge of power that will come to you with which to meet all your problems will be past all understanding.

In Chapter 3 we have tried to make plain the way to get God into the centre of our lives. Some of us have always thought prayer was confined to the church, and, perhaps, to going to bed at night. We've not thought of prayer as something that goes on in us all the time. Every thought of God is a prayer: every reaching out to Him for help is a prayer. You can talk with God at any minute anywhere.

But for the accomplishment of that for which we pray, we have to do more than ask for it. We have to reach out a hand to receive it. We have to believe that we will receive it. We have to believe, even if nothing happens for quite a while. We have to control our own thoughts and imagination to the extent of counting on it, planning on it, getting ready for it. It will come.

Chapter 4 was on the subject of making your own happiness. Really, if we have learned to pray and believe, to have faith in ourselves and in God, we will have come a long way toward happiness. If we expect happiness, it will come. Things don't make us happy. The circumstances of our lives don't make us happy. Your happiness depends primarily on the kind of inner life you live. And that life depends on how close you live to God. There's your answer.

Our next chapter, the fifth, had to do with the kind of boy or girl I'm sure you aren't: the kind who stews and frets, finds fault and grumbles; the kind for whom nothing is ever quite right. For there is nothing at all to be done with a young person like that except to make him over: change him from the bottom up, from inside out. And this kind of person is often the result of modern improvements. If the radio didn't blare at him, if television didn't dance and scream at him, if airplanes didn't zing over him and auto horns didn't blat—if the telephone didn't ring or the front doorbell summon him—then perhaps he'd hear the birds sing. He might even see how utterly entrancing is a spring day with its greens and whites and reds and blues; he might look up at the sky and stop to watch the cloud formations. If he lived that kind of life, he'd not growl and grump around home; he'd not quarrel with his classmates. He'd not talk impudently to the teacher or to his parents, He'd probably be a very pleasant boy—or girl—to have around.

But we can't do a thing about modern gadgets. They're here to stay so we have to learn to live with them. We have to learn that in God there is quietness; in God there is peace. Every time we are tempted to be nervous, annoyed, we can turn to God. In contemplating Him and His peace we become peaceful. That's all there is to it.

Chapter 6 is one of my favourite themes. I like to talk about it; I like to see people practise it. None of us knows his own powers. All we know is that they are far more extensive than we have the imagination to compass. Abraham Lincoln was a storekeeper; yet he became America's foremost citizen. Herbert Hoover was a poor Quaker lad who had to work hard to get an education. But he became not only a President of the United States but an outstanding engineer in a world of eminent engineers.

You can be what you want to be. Only you have to want it enough, and you have to use the help God gives you to release the powers that lie dormant within you. To be sure there's a price to be paid. If you want to lead your class, God can't be expected to do it for you. You have to co-operate: you have to stay at home and study when the family is going to a movie you want to see; you have to go to bed early and get a proper amount of sleep in order to feel fresh and rested in the morning when you may have wanted to see a late programme on television. But whatever you want more than you want anything else in life, that you can have: if God goes along with you, wants it for you, gives you His strength and Power.

"Be a Winner." (Chapter 7) You can be if you want to be. But you have to want it and believe that it is possible. Thoughts of failure bring failure: thoughts of success bring success. Tell yourself you believe that until you find that you do believe it. Tell yourself what it is that you want: tell God about it; believe that He will help you; listen to His advice and follow it. It's that simple.

Chapter 8, "Why Worry?" If God is with you,

you've nothing to worry about. Your problem is to see to it that He is with you.

In Chapter 9 we have offered ten different ways to help you solve your problems. Try them: they'll help. But the sum and substance is this: believe that there is a solution; then with the help of God find that solution.

"What to Do in a Slump." (Chapter 10) Those are periods we all have. And we all have different ways of meeting the crisis. The most common practice is to sink into depression; enjoy our misery. The reasons for these low spots in our lives are many and the way out is always the same. Simply pray that Jesus Christ will give us healing for our faults of disposition.

The next chapter, Chapter 11, I consider very important. "You Are What You Think." So many do not realise the truth of that. They think they are what they are as a result of inherited characteristics plus the haphazard circumstances of their environment. They admit that effort on their part may change some of those native characteristics, may modify in some degree their environmental state but for the most part they are what they were born to be.

That isn't so. Your thoughts are more powerful than your environment, more powerful than your inherited characteristics. Your mind is your own you can let destructive elements live there and make you less than your best; you can throw them out and

let God in and be what He intends you to be. Your
uture is entirely in your own hands; that is to say,
n the keeping of your own mind. You can be what
ou think.

Chapter 12, "Easy Does It." Believe it. It takes all
he strain out of living. Whatever your problem,
nental or physical, you can solve it the easy way.
Tackle everything with muscles relaxed, with your
iervous system relaxed. We can tighten up physi-
ally and mentally and defeat ourselves. Or we can
emove the tension and let the power flow: God's
ower, which He gives us.

The problem of being liked, discussed in Chapter
3, is one with which we have all dealt. We can say
ve don't care. We can try for popularity by "yes"-ing
verybody. But the simple answer is that people like
ou when you like them: honestly, sincerely like
iem. And that means thinking about other people
istead of ourselves; being more interested in their
roblems than in our own; being willing to listen
istead of talk. You can't? Try! Difficult? Of
ourse!

Through the help of God, through courage,
iaracter, manliness, and the power of positive
iinking you can make your life whatever you want
to be.

Epilogue

You have finished this book. What have you read?

Simply a series of practical and workable techniques for living a successful life. You have read a formula of belief and practice which should help you win victory over defeat.

Examples have been given, many of them of young people about your age, of those who have believed and applied the suggestions given here. These stories have been told to demonstrate that by using the same methods you can obtain the same results.

But reading is not enough. If you really hope to attain a successful life, please go back and practise persistently the suggestions given. Keep at it. Th results will come.

I have written this book in a sincere desire to help you. It will give me great happiness to know that th book has helped you. I have absolute confidence an belief in the principles outlined in this volume. They have been tested in the laboratory of spiritual experience and practical demonstration. They wor when worked.

We may never meet in person, but in this book we have met. We are spiritual friends. I pray for you. God will help you—so believe and live successfully.

NORMAN VINCENT PEALE